Vision and Prophecy
The Spirit of Truth: The Voice of the Bridegroom

by

Daniel Timothy Bridegroom

DORRANCE PUBLISHING CO
EST. 1920
PITTSBURGH, PENNSYLVANIA 15238

Dorrance Publishing Co
585 Alpha Drive
Pittsburgh, PA 15238
Visit our website at *www.dorrancebookstore.com*

ISBN: 978-1-6853-7444-0
eISBN: 978-1-6853-7588-1

Jeremiah 30:2: "Thus speaks The Lord God of Israel, saying: 'Write in a book for yourself all the words that I have spoken to you.' 3 'For Behold The Days are coming' says the Lord, 'That I will bring back from captivity My People Israel and Judah,' says the Lord, 'And I will cause them to Return to the land that I gave to their fathers, and they shall possess it.'"

5 "For thus says The Lord: 'We have heard a voice of trembling, of fear, and not of peace.' 15 'Why do you cry about your afflictions? Your sorrow is incurable. Because of the multitude of your iniquities. Because your sins have increased, I have done these things to you.' 23 'Behold, the whirlwind of The Lord goes forth with fury, a continuing whirlwind where it shall fall violently on the heads of the wicked.' 24 'The Fierce Anger of The Lord will not return until He has done it, and until he has performed the intent of His Heart. In the Latter Days you will consider it.'"

31:2: "Thus says The Lord: 'The People who survived The Sword found grace in the wilderness—Israel, when I went to give him rest.' 3 The Lord has appeared of old to me, saying: 'Yes, I have loved you with an everlasting love; therefore, with lovingkindness I have drawn you. 6 For there shall be A Day when the watchmen will cry on Mount Ephraim, 'Arise, and let us go up to Zion, to The Lord our God." 12 Therefore they shall come and sing in the height of Zion, Streaming to The Goodness of The Lord—for wheat and new wine and oil, for the young of the flock and the herd; their souls shall be like a well-watered garden, and they shall sorrow no more at all. 34 "No more shall every an teach his neighbor, and every man his brother, saying, 'Know The Lord!' 'For they all shall know Me, from the least of them, to the greatest of them says The Lord, For I will forgive their iniquity, and their sin I will remember no more."

33:9: "Then it shall be to Me a name of joy, a praise, and an honor before all nations of the earth, who shall hear all the good that I do to them; they shall fear and tremble for all the goodness and all the prosperity that I provide for it." 10 "Thus says The Lord; 'Again there shall be heard in This Place—of which you say, "It shall be desolate, without man and without beast'—in the cities of Judah, in the streets of Jerusalem that are desolate, without man and without inhabitant and without beast, 11 'The Voice of Joy and The Voice of Gladness, The Voice of The Bridegroom and The Voice of The Bride, And The Voice of those who will say; "Praise The Lord of hosts, for The Lord is good, for His mercy endures forever"—and of those who bring The Sacrifice of Praise into The House of The Lord. For I will cause the captives of the land to return as at the first,' says The Lord. Psalms 105:8: He remembered His Covenant forever, The Word which He commanded, for a thousand generations. 9 The Covenant which He made with Abraham, and His Oath to Isaac, 10 And confirmed it to Jacob for A Statute, to Israel as An Everlasting Covenant, 11 Saying; "To you I will give the land of Canaan as the allotment of your inheritance."

Psalms 106:2: Who can utter The Mighty Acts of The Lord? Who can declare all His praise? Blessed are those who keep justice, and he who does righteousness at all time! 4 Remember me, O Lord, with the favor you have toward Your people. Oh, visit me with Your Salvation. 5 That I may see the benefit of Your Chosen Ones, that I may rejoice in the gladness of Your nation, that I may glory with Your Inheritance.

Psalms 106:8: Nevertheless He saved them for His name's sake, that He might make His Mighty Power known. 10 He saved them from the hand of him who hated them and redeemed them from the hand of the enemy. 11 The waters covered their enemies; there was not one of them left. 12 Then they believed His Words; they sang His Praise.

Micah 4:8: And You, O Tower of The Flock, the stronghold of The Daughters of Zion, to you shall it come, even The Former Dominion shall come, The Kingdom of The Daughter of Jerusalem. 11 Now also many nations have gathered against You, who say, "Let her be defiled, and let our eyes look upon Zion." 12 But they do not know The Thoughts of The Lord, nor do they understand His Counsel; for He will gather them like sheaves to the threshing floor. 13 "Arise and thresh, O Daughter of Zion; for I will make your horn iron, and I will make your hooves bronze, you shall beat in pieces many people; I will consecrate their gain to The Lord, and their substance to The Lord of The Whole Earth."

Ezekiel 37:22: "And I will make them One Nation in the land, on the mountains of Israel and One King shall be King over them all; they shall no longer be two nations, nor shall they ever be divided into two kingdoms again. 23 They shall not defile themselves anymore with their idols, nor with their detestable things, nor with any of their transgressions; but I will deliver them from all their dwelling places in which they have sinned and will cleanse them. Then shall they be My People and I will be their God. 28 The nations also will know that I, The Lord sanctify Israel. when My Sanctuary is in their midst forevermore."

Isaiah 64:1: Oh, that You would rend the heavens! That You would come down! That the mountains might shake at Your Presence—2 As fire burns brushwood, as fire causes water to boil—to make Your Name known to Your adversaries, that the nations may tremble at Your Presence! 4 For since The Beginning of the world men have not heard nor perceived by the ear, nor has the eye seen any God besides You, who acts for the one who waits for Him. 5 You meet him who rejoices and does righteousness, who remembers You in Your Ways, You are indeed angry, for we have sinned—in these ways we continue; and we need to be saved.

Isaiah 65:2: I have stretched out My Hands all day long to a rebellious people, who walk in a way that is not good, according to their own thoughts: 5 Who say, "Keep to Yourself, do not come near me, for I am holier than You!' These are smoke in My nostrils, a fire that burns all the day. 6 "Behold, it is written before Me: I will not keep silence, but will repay—even repay into their bosom—Isaiah 65:12: Therefore I will number you for The Sword, and you shall all bow down to The Slaughter; because when I called, you did not answer; when I spoke, you did not hear, but did evil before My Eyes, and 'chose' that in which I do not delight."

17 "For behold, I create new heavens and A New Earth; and the former shall not be remembered or come to mind." 24 "It shall come to pass that before they call, I will answer; and while they are still speaking, I will hear." 25 The wolf and the lamb shall feed together, the lion shall eat straw like the ox, and the dust shall be the serpents food. They shall not hurt nor destroy in all My Holy Mountain," says The Lord.

Isaiah 66:6: The sound of noise from the city! A voice from the temple! The Voice of The Lord, who fully repays His enemies! 16 For by fire and by His Sword The Lord will judge all flesh; and the slain of The Lord shall be many. 18 "For I know their works and their thoughts. It shall be that I will gather all nations and tongues; and they shall come and see My Glory." 23 And it shall come to pass that from one new moon to another, and from one Sabbath to another, all flesh shall come to worship before Me," says The Lord.

Zechariah 8:4: "Thus says The Lord of hosts: 'Old men and old women shall again sit in The Streets of Jerusalem, each one with his staff in his hand because of great age. 5 The Streets of The City shall be full of boys and girls playing in its streets.' 8 I will bring them back, and they shall dwell in the midst of Jerusalem. They shall be My People and I will be their God, in Truth and Righteousness.' 12:10: "And I will pour on The House of David and on the inhabitants of Jerusalem 'The Spirit' of grace and supplication; then they will look on Me whom they pierced. Yes, they will mourn for Him as one mourns for his only son and grieve for Him as one grieves for a firstborn.

13:8: And it shall come to pass in all the land, says The Lord, "That two-thirds in it shall be cut off and die, but one-third shall be left in it: 9 I will bring the one-third through the fire, will refine them as silver is refined, and test them as gold is tested. They will call on My Name, and I will answer them, I will say, 'This is My People'; and each one will say, "The Lord is my God." 14:7: It shall be one day which is known to The Lord—neither day nor night. But at evening time it shall happen that it will be light. 8 And in that day it shall be that Living Waters shall flow from Jerusalem, half of them toward the eastern sea and half of them toward the western sea; in both summer and winter it shall occur.

Malachi 1:6: "A son honors his father, and a servant his master. If then I am The Father, where is My honor? And if I am A Master, where is My reverence? says The Lord of hosts to you priests who despise My Name. Yet you say, 'In what way have we despised Your Name?' 7 "You offer defiled food on My altar, but say, 'In what way have we defiled You? 'By saying, 'The table of The Lord is contemptible.' 8 And when you offer the blind as a sacrifice, is it not evil? And when you offer the lame and sick, is it not evil? Offer it then to your governor! Would he be pleased with you? Would he accept you favorably?" says The Lord of hosts.

Jeremiah 33:14: "'Behold, the days are coming,' says The Lord, 'that I will perform that Good Thing which I have promised to The House of Israel and to The House of Judah:' 15 'In those days and at that time I will cause to grow up to David a Branch of Righteousness; He shall execute judgment and righteousness in the earth. II Samuel 7:25: "Now, O Lord God, The Word which You have spoken concerning His House, establish it forever and do as You have said."

II Kings 19:30: 'And the remnant who have escaped of The House of Judah shall again take root downward, and bear fruit upward. 31 For out of Jerusalem shall go a remnant, and those who escape from Mount Zion. The Zeal of The Lord of hosts will do this. 34 'For I will defend this city, to save it for My own sake, and for My servant David's sake.'

Psalms 99:1: The Lord reigns, let the people tremble! He dwells between the cherubim; let the earth be moved! 2 The Lord is great in Zion, and He is high above all the peoples. Psalms 146:5: Happy is he who has The God of Jacob for his help, whose hope is in The Lord his God. 6 Who made the heaven and earth, the sea, and all that is in them, who keeps Truth forever. 7 Who executes justice for the oppressed, who gives food to the hungry. The Lord gives freedom to the prisoners.

8 The Lord opens the eyes of the blind; The Lord raises those who are bowed down; The Lord loves the righteous. 9 The Lord watches over the strangers; He relieves the fatherless and widow; but the way of the wicked He turns upside down. 10 The Lord shall reign forever— Your God, O Zion, to all generations, Praise The Lord! Psalms 149:2: Let Israel rejoice in their Maker; let The Children of Zion be joyful in their King. 4 For The Lord takes pleasure in His People; He will beautify the humble with Salvation.

Proverbs 3:1: My Son, do not forget My Law, but let your heart keep My Commands: 2 For 'Length of Days and Long Life and Peace' they will add to you. 5 Trust in The Lord with all your heart, an lean not on your own understanding. 6 In all your way acknowledge Him, and He shall direct your paths. 7 Do not be wise in your own eyes; Fear The Lord and depart from evil.

Malachi 4:1: "For behold, 'The Day' is coming, burning like an oven, and all the proud, yes, all who do wickedly will be stubble. And 'The Day' which is coming shall burn them up," says The Lord of hosts, "that will leave them neither root nor branch. 2 But to you who fear

My Name, 'The Son of Righteousness' shall arise with healing in His wings; and you shall go out and grow fat like stallfed calves.

Proverbs 10:27: The Fear of The Lord prolongs days, but the years of the wicked will be shortened. 30 The righteous will never be removed, but the wicked will not inherit the earth. 11:3: The integrity of the Upright will guide them, but the perversity of the unfaithful will destroy them. 11 By The Blessing of The Upright the city is exalted, but it is overthrown by the mouth of the wicked.

Proverbs 12:22: Lying lips are an abomination to The Lord, but those who deal truthfully are His delight. 27 The lazy man does not roast what he took in hunting, but 'Diligence' is man's precious possession. 13:2: A man shall eat well by the fruit of his mouth, but 'the soul' of the unfaithful feeds on violence. 10 By pride comes nothing but strife, but with the well-advised is wisdom. 13 He who despises 'The Word' will be destroyed, but he who fears the commandment will be rewarded. 24 He who spares his rod hates his son, but he who loves him disciplines him promptly.

Proverbs 14:5: A faithful witness does not lie, but a false witness will utter lies. 14 The backslider in heart will be filled with his own ways, but a good man will be satisfied from above. 16 A wise man fears and departs from evil, but a fool rages and is self-confident. 25 A true witness delivers souls, but a deceitful witness speaks lies.

Ezra 9:6: And I said: "O My God, I am too ashamed and humiliated to lift up My Face to You, My God; for our iniquities have risen higher than our heads, and our guilt has grown up to the heavens." 7 "Since the days of our fathers to 'This Day' we have been very guilty, for our iniquities we, our kings, and our priests have been delivered into the hand of the kings of the lands, to The Sword, to captivity, to plunder, and to humiliation, as it is 'This Day.' 8 And now for 'A Little While' Grace has been shown from The Lord our God, to leave us a remnant to escape, and to give us 'A Peg' in His Holy Place, that 'Our God' may 'Enlighten' our eyes and give us 'A Measure of Revival' in our bondage.

Psalms 10:12: Arise, O Lord! O God, lift up Your Hand! Do not forget the humble. 13 Why do the wicked renounce God? He has said in his heart, "You will not require an account." 14 But You have seen, for You observe trouble and grief, to repay it by Your Hand. The helpless commits himself to You; You are the helper of the fatherless. 17 Lord,

You have heard the desire of the humble; You will prepare their heart; You will cause Your ear to hear, 18 To do justice to the fatherless and the oppressed, that 'The Man of The Earth' may oppress no more.

Ecclesiastes 8:9: All this I have seen, and applied my heart to every work that is done under the sun; there is a time in which one man rules over another to his own hurt. 9:2: All things come alike to all; one event happens to the righteous and the wicked; to the good, the clean, and the unclean; to him who sacrifices and him who does not sacrifice. As is the good, so is the sinner; he who takes an oath as he who fears an oath. Isaiah 14:26: This is the purpose that is purposed against the whole earth, and this is 'The Hand' that is stretched out over all the nations. 27 For The Lord of hosts has purposed, and who will annul it? His Hand is stretched out, and who will turn It back?

Psalms 36:1: An oracle within my heart concerning the transgression of the wicked: there is no fear of God before his eyes. 2 For he flatters himself in his own eyes, when he finds out his iniquity and when he hates. 3 The words of his mouth are wickedness and deceit; he has ceased to be wise and to do good. 4 He devises wickedness on his bed, he set himself in a way that is not good, he does not abhor evil.

Job 20:2: "Therefore my anxious thoughts make me answer, because of the turmoil within me. 3 I have heard the rebuke that reproaches me, and 'The Spirit' of my understanding causes me to answer. 4 "Do you not know this of old, since man was placed on earth, 5 That the triumphing of the wicked is short, and the joy of the hypocrite is but for a moment? 21:24: Yet they say to God, 'Depart from us, for we do not desire 'The Knowledge of Your Ways.' 15 Who is The Almighty, that we should serve Him? And what profit do we have if we pray to Him?

Job 22:4: Is it because of your fear of Him that He corrects you, and enters into judgment with you? 5 Is not your wickedness great, and your iniquity without end? 15 Will you keep to the old way which wicked men have trod, 16 Who were cut down before their time, whose foundations were swept away by 'A Flood'? 21 "Now acquaint yourself with Him, and be at peace; thereby good will come to you. 22 Receive, Please, instruction from His mouth, and lay up His Words in your heart. 26 For then you will have your delight in The Almighty and lift up your face to God.

Micah 7:7: Therefore I will look to The Lord; I will wait for 'The God of My Salvation': My God will hear me. 8 Do not rejoice over me, my enemy; when I fall, I will Arise; when I set in darkness, The Lord will be A Light to me. 9 I will bear 'The Indignation of The Lord,' because I have sinned against Him, until He pleads 'My Case' and executes justice for me. He will bring me forth to 'The Light': I will see His Righteousness.

10 The she who is my enemy will see, and shame will cover her who said to me, "Where is The Lord your God?" My eyes will see her; now she will be trampled down like mud in the streets, 11 In the day when your walls are to be built, in that day 'The Decree' shall go far and wide. 12 In that day they shall come to You from Assyria and the fortified cities, from the fortress to the river, from sea to sea, and mountain to mountain. 13 Yet the land shall be desolate because of those who dwell in it, and for the fruit of their deeds. 16 The nations shall see and be ashamed of all their might; they shall put their hand over their mouth; their ears shall be deaf. 17 They shall lick the dust like a serpent; they shall crawl from the holes like snakes of the earth. They shall be afraid of The Lord our God and shall fear because of You.

18 Who is a God like You, pardoning iniquity and passing over the transgression of the remnant of His heritage? He does not retain His Anger forever, because He delights in mercy. 19 He will again have compassion on us and will subdue our iniquities. You will cast all our sins into the depths of the sea. Micah 7:20: You will give Truth to Jacob and mercy to Abraham, which You have sworn to our fathers from days of old.

Nahum 3:1: Woe to the bloody city! It is all full of lies and robbery, its victim never departs. 4 Because of the multitude of harlotries of the seductive harlot, the mistress of sorceries, who sale nations through her harlotries, and families through her sorceries. Jermiah 25:31: A noise will come to 'The Ends of The Earth—for The Lord has a controversy with the nations; He will plead 'His Case' with all flesh. He will give those who are wicked to 'The Sword'; says The Lord.

Job 32:7: I said, 'Age should speak, and multitude of years should teach wisdom.' 8 But there is 'A Spirit' in man, and The Breath of The Almighty gives him understanding. 9 Great men are not always wise, nor do the aged always understand justice. 11 Indeed I waited for your words, I listened to your reasonings, while you searched out what to say. 18 For I am full of words; 'The Spirit' within me compels me.

Job 33:3: My words come from my Upright heart; my lips utter pure knowledge. 4 'The Spirit of God' has made me, and 'The Breath of The Almighty' gives me life. 5 If you can answer me, set your words in order before me; take your stand. 6 Truly I am as your spokesman before God; I also have been formed out of clay. 12 "Look, in 'This' you are not righteous. I will answer you, For God is greater than man. 13 Why do you contend with Him? For He does not give an accounting of any of His Words. 16 Then he opens the ears of men and seals their instruction. 17 In order to turn man from his deed and conceal pride from man. 18 He keeps his soul from the pit, and his life from perishing by 'The Sword.'

Psalms 125:1: Those who trust in The Lord are like Mount Zion, which cannot be moved, but abides forever. 3 For the scepter of wickedness shall not rest on the land allotted to the righteous, lest the righteous reach out their hand to iniquity. 4 Do good, O Lord, to those who are good, and to those who are Upright in their hearts. Ezekiel 36:28: "Then you shall dwell in the land that I gave your fathers; you shall be My People, and I will be your God."

Ezekiel 38:8: "After many days you will be visited. In 'The Latter Years' you will come into the land of those brought back from The Sword and gathered from many people on The Mountain of Israel, which had long been desolate; they were brought out of the nations, and now all of them dwell safely." 39:7: "So I will make 'My Holy Name' known in the midst of My People Israel, and I will not let them profane 'My Holy Name' anymore. Then the nations shall know that I Am The Lord, The Holy One of Israel." 8 "Surely it is coming, and it shall be done,' says The Lord God. This is 'The Day' of which I have spoken."

Exodus 31:16: Therefore The Children of Israel shall keep 'The Sabbath,' to observe 'The Sabbath" throughout their generations as 'A Perpetual Covenant.' 17 'It is a sign between Me and The Children of Israel forever; for in six days The Lord made the heavens and the earth, and on the seventh day He rested and was refreshed.'"

Exodus 32:7: And The Lord said to Moses, "Go, get down! For your people whom you brought out of the land of Egypt have corrupted themselves. 9 And The Lord said to Moses, "I have seen this people, and indeed it is a stiff-necked people!" 33 And The Lord said to Moses, "Whoever has sinned against Me, I will blot him out of 'My Book.'" 33:11: So The Lord spoke to Moses face to face, as a man speaks to his friend. And he would return to the camp, but his servant Joshua the son of Nun, a young man, did not depart from the tabernacle. 34:10: And He said: "Behold, I made a Covenant, before all your people I will do marvels such as have not been done in all the earth, nor in any nation; and all the people among whom you are shall see 'The Work of The Lord.' For it is an awesome thing that I will do with you."

Jeremiah 20:7: O Lord, You induced me, and I was persuaded; You are stronger than I, and have prevailed. I am in derision daily; everyone mocks me. 8 For when I spoke, I cried out; I shouted, "violence and plunder!" Because "The Word of The Lord' was made to me a reproach and a derision daily. 9 Then I said, "I will not make mention of Him, nor speak anymore in 'His Name.'" But 'His Word' was in my heart like a burning fire shut up in my bones; I was weary of holding it back, and I could not. 10 For I heard many mocking: "Fear on every side!" "Report, they say, and we will report it!" All my acquaintances watched for my stumbling, saying, "Perhaps he can be induced; then we will prevail against him, and we will take our revenge on him."

20:11: But The Lord is with me as a Mighty, Awesome One. Therefore, my persecutors will stumble and will not prevail. They will be greatly ashamed, for they will not prosper. Their everlasting confusion will never be forgotten. 12 But, O Lord of hosts, You who test the righteous, and see the mind and heart, let me see 'Your Vengeance' on them; for I have pleaded 'My Cause' before You.

I Timothy 2:5: For there is One God and One Mediator between God and man. The Man Jesus Christ, 6 Who gave Himself 'A Ransom' for all, to be testified in 'Due Time.' 7 For which I was appointed A Preacher and an Apostle—I am speaking 'The Truth' in Christ and not lying—A teacher of the Gentiles in 'Faith' and 'Truth.'

Proverbs 2:1: My Son, if you receive 'My Words,' and treasure 'My Commands' within you. 2 So that you incline your ear to wisdom and apply your heart to understanding; 5 Then you will understand 'The Fear of The Lord,' and find 'The Knowledge of God.' 10 When wisdom enters your heart, and knowledge is pleasant to your soul, 11 Discretion will preserve you, understanding will keep you, 12 To deliver you from the way of evil, from the man who speaks perverse things. 13 From those who leave 'The Paths of Righteousness' to walk in the ways of darkness, 14 Who rejoice in doing evil, and delight in the perversity of the wicked; 15 Whose ways are crooked, and who are devious in their paths.

Psalms 10:3: For the wicked boasts of his heart's desire; he blesses the greedy and renounces The Lord. 7 His mouth is full of cursing and deceit and oppression; under his tongue is trouble and iniquity. 8 He sits in the lurking places of the villages; in secret places he murders the innocent; his eyes are secretly fixed on the helpless. 11 He has said in his heart, "God has forgotten; He hides His face; He will never see."

Psalms 35:1: Plead 'My Cause,' O Lord, with those who strive with me, fight against those who fight against me. 2 Take hold of shield and buckler and stand up for my help. I John 2:18: Little children, it is 'The Last hour' and as you have heard that the antichrist is coming, even now 'many' antichrists have come, by which we know that it is 'The Last Hour.' 22 Who is a liar but he who denies that Jesus is 'The Christ'? He is antichrist who denies 'The Father' and 'The Son.'

I John 2:26: These things I have written to you concerning those who try to deceive you. 3:8: He who sins is of the devil, for the devil has sinned from the beginning. For this purpose, 'The Son of God' was manifested, that He might destroy the works of the devil.

Genesis 6:5: Then The Lord saw that the wickedness of man was great in the earth, and that every intent of the thoughts of his heart was only evil continually. 6 And The Lord was sorry that He made man on the earth, and He was grieved in His heart. 12 So God looked upon the earth, and indeed it was corrupt; for all flesh had corrupted their way on the earth.

Job 15:4: Yes, you cast off fear, and restrain prayer before God. 5 For your iniquity teaches your mouth, and 'you choose' the tongue of the crafty. 6 Your own mouth condemns you, and not I; yes, your own lips testify against you. 12 Why does your heart carry you away, 13 That you turn your spirit against God, and let such words go out of your mouth? 16:2: "I have heard many such things; miserable comforters are you all!"

Job 19:23: "Oh, that My Words were written! Oh, that they were inscribed in 'A Book'! 24 That they were engraved on 'A Rock' with an iron pen and lead, forever!" 25 For I know that 'My Redeemer' lives, and He shall stand at last on the earth; 26 And after my skin is destroyed, this I know, that in my flesh I shall see God. 27 Whom I shall see for myself, and my eyes shall behold, and not another. How my heart yearns within me!

Psalms 71:1: In You, O Lord, I put my trust; let me never be put to shame. 2 Deliver me in 'Your Righteousness' and cause me to escape; incline You ear to me and save me. 7 I have become as a wonder to many, but You are 'My Strong Refuge.' 15 My mouth shall tell of 'Your Righteousness and Your Salvation' all the day. For I do not know their limits. 16 I will go in 'The Strength of The Lord God'; I will make mention of 'Your Righteousness,' of Yours only.

17 O God, You have taught me from my youth; and to 'This Day' I declare Your wondrous works. 18 Now also when I am old and grey-headed, O God, do not forsake me, until I declare 'Your Strength' to 'This' generation, 'Your Power' to everyone 'who is to come.' 20 You, who have shown me great and severe troubles, shall 'Revive Me' again, and bring me up again from the depths of the earth.

Psalms 72:3: The mountains will bring peace to the people, and the little hills, by Righteousness. 4 He will bring justice to the poor of the people; He will save the children of the needy and will break in pieces the oppressor. 7 In 'His Days' the righteous shall flourish, and abundance of peace, until the moon is no more. 8 He shall have dominion also from sea to sea, and from "The River' to The End of The Earth.'

Ezekiel 44:23: "And they shall teach My People the difference between the holy and the unholy and cause them to discern between the unclean and the clean." 24 "In controversy they shall stand as judges and judge it according to 'My Judgments.'" They shall keep 'My Laws and My Statutes' in all My Appointed Meetings, and they shall hallow 'My Sabbaths.'"

Psalms 28:1: To You I will cry, O Lord my Rock; do not be silent to me, lest, if You are silent to me, I become like those who go down to the pit. 3 Do not take me away with the wicked and with the workers of iniquity, who speak peace to the neighbors, but evil is in their heart. 4 Give them according to their deeds, and according to the wickedness of their endeavors; give them according to the work of their hands; render to them what they deserve.

Proverbs 20:9: Who can say, "I have made my heart clean, I am pure from my sin"? 11 Even a child is known by his deeds, whether what he does is pure and right. 34 A man's steps are of The Lord; how then can a man understand his own way? 26 A wise king sifts out the wicked and brings the threshing wheel over them. 28 Mercy and 'Truth' preserve the king, and by lovingkindness he upholds his throne.

Proverbs 21:11: When the scoffer is punished, the simple is made wise; but when the wise is instructed, he receives knowledge. 24 A proud and haughty man—"Scoffer" is his name; he acts with arrogant pride. 22:10: Cast out the scoffer, and contention will leave; yes, strife and reproach will cease. 17 Incline your ear and hear 'The Words of The Wise' and apply your heart to My knowledge. 18 For it is a pleasant thing if you keep them within you; let them all be fixed upon your lips. 19 So that your trust may be in The Lord; I have instructed you 'Today,' even you.

20 Have I not written to you excellent things of counsels and knowledge, 21 That I may make you know the certainty of "The Words of Truth." 23:12 Apply your heart to instruction and your ears to words of knowledge. 13 Do not withhold correction from a child, for if you beat him with a rod, he will not die. 14 You shall beat him with a rod and deliver his soul from hell. 18 For surely there is a hereafter, and your hope will not be cut off.

Job 5:1: "Call out now;" is there anyone who will answer you? And to which of 'The Holy Ones' will you turn? 2 For wrath kills the foolish man, and envy slays a simple one. 8 "But as for me, I would seek God, and to God I would commit 'My Cause'—Luke 1:1: Inasmuch as many have taken in hand to set in order a narrative of those things which have been fulfilled among us. 2 Just as those who from the beginning were eyewitnesses and ministers of 'The Word' delivered them to us.

Luke 1:68: "Blessed is The Lord God of Israel, for He has visited and redeemed His People, 69 And has raised up A Horn of Salvation for us in The House of His servant David, 70 As He spoke by the mouth of His holy prophets, who have been since the world began. 71 That we should be saved from our enemies and from the hand of all who hate us, 72 To perform the mercy promised to our fathers and to remember His Holy Covenant. 73 The oath which He swore to our father Abraham: 74 To grant us that we, being delivered from the hand of our enemies, might serve Him without fear. 75 In holiness and righteousness before Him all the days of our life.

Psalms 3:1: Lord, how they have increased who trouble me! Many are they who rise up against me! 2 Many are they who say of me, "There is no help for Him in God." Selah (chosen future) Psalms 4:2: How long, O you sons of man, will you turn 'My Glory' into shame? How long will you love worthlessness and seek falsehood? Selah Psalms 5:10: Pronounce them guilty, O God! Let them fall by their own counsels; cast them out in the multitude of their transgressions, for they have rebelled against You.

Psalms 6:8: Depart from me, all you workers of iniquity; For The Lord has heard the voice of my weeping. 9 The Lord has heard my supplication; The Lord will receive my prayer. 10 Let all my enemies be ashamed and greatly troubled; let them turn back and be ashamed suddenly. 9:3: When my enemies turn back, they shall fall and perish at Your Presence. 8 He shall judge the world in righteousness, and He shall administer judgment for the peoples in 'Uprightness.'

Psalms 9:11: Sing praise to The Lord, who dwells in Zion! Declare His deeds among the people. 11:6: Upon the wicked He will rain coals; fire and brimstone and a burning wind shall be the portion of their cup. Jeremiah 25:31: A noise will come to the ends of the earth—for The Lord has a controversy with the nations; He will plead 'His Case' with all flesh. He will give those who are wicked to 'The Sword,' says The Lord."

32 Thus says The Lord of hosts: Behold, disaster shall go forth from nation to nation, and a great whirlwind shall be raised up from the farthest parts of the earth. Jeremiah 25:33: "And at 'That Day' the slain of The Lord shall be from one end of earth even to the other end of the earth. They shall not be lamented, or gathered, or buried; they shall become refuse on the ground.

34 "Wail, shepherds, and cry! Roll about in the ashes, you leaders of the flock! For the days of your slaughter and your dispersions are fulfilled; you shall fall like a precious vessel. 35 And the shepherds will have no way to flee, nor the leaders of the flock to escape. 36 A voice of the cry of the shepherds, and a wailing of the leaders to the flock will be heard. For The Lord has plundered their pasture. 37 And the peaceful dwellings are cut down because of The Fierce Anger of The Lord.

Jeremiah 26:13: "Now therefore, amend your ways and your doings, and obey 'The Voice of The Lord your God'; then The Lord will relent concerning 'The Doom' that He has pronounced against you. 27:5: 'I have made the earth, the man and the beast that are on the ground, by My Great Power and by My Outstretched Arm, and have given it to whom it seemed proper to Me. 29:11: For I know the thoughts that I think toward you, says The Lord, thoughts of peace and not of evil, to give you a future and a hope.

Psalms 106:21: They forgot God their Savior, who had done great things in Egypt. 26 Therefore He raised up His Hand in an oath against them, to overthrow them in the wilderness, 28 They joined themselves also to Baal of Peor, and ate sacrifices made to the dead. 29 Thus they provoked Him to anger with their deeds, and the plague broke out among them. 33 Because they rebelled against 'His Spirit,' so that He spoke rashly with His lips. 35 But they mingled with the Gentiles and learned their works. 41 And He gave then into the hand of the Gentiles, and those who hated them ruled over them.

Jeremiah 8:5: Why has this people slidden back, Jerusalem. in 'A Perpetual Backsliding'? They hold fast to deceit; they refuse to return. 6 I listen and heard, but they do not speak 'Aright.' No man repented of his wickedness, saying, 'What have I done?' Everyone turned to his own course, as the horse rushes into battle. 7 Even the stork in the heavens know her appointed times; and the turtledove, the swift, and the swallow observe the time of their coming. But My People do not know 'The Judgment of The Lord.'

8 "How can you say, 'We are wise, and The Law of The Lord is with us; Look, the false pen of the scribe certainly works falsehood. 9 The wise men are ashamed, they are dismayed and taken. Behold, they have rejected 'The Word of The Lord; so what wisdom do they have? 11 For they have healed the hurt of The Daughter of My People slightly, saying, 'Peace, Peace!' when there is no peace.

12 Were they ashamed when they committed abomination? No! They were not at all ashamed, nor did they know how to blush. Therefore, they shall fall among those who fall; in 'The Time' of their punishment they shall be cast down," says The Lord. 15 "We looked for peace, but no good came; and for a time of health, and there was trouble! 22 Is there no balm in Gilead, Is there no physician there? Why then is there no recovery for the health of The Daughter of My People?

Jeremiah 9:2: Oh, that I had in the wilderness a lodging place for travelers; that I might leave My People and go from them! For they are all adulterers, an assembly of treacherous men. 3 "And like their bow they have bent their tongues for lies. They are not valiant for The Truth on the earth. For they proceed from evil to evil, and they do not know me," says The Lord. 5 Everyone will deceive his neighbor and will not speak 'The Truth'; they have taught their tongue to speak lies; weary themselves to commit iniquity. 6 Your dwelling place is in the midst of deceit; through deceit they refuse to know Me,' says The Lord.

19 For a voice of wailing is heard from Zion; 'How we are plundered! We are greatly ashamed because we have forsaken the land, because we have been cast out of our dwellings.'" 21 For death has come through our windows, has entered our palaces, to kill off the children— No longer to be outside! and the young men—no longer on the streets! 22 Speak, "Thus says The Lord: 'Even the carcasses of men shall fall as refuse on the open field, like cuttings after the harvester, and no one shall gather them.'"

10:2: Thus says The Lord: "Do not learn the way of the Gentiles; Do not be dismayed at the signs of heaven, for the Gentiles are dismayed at them. Joel 3:14: Multitudes, multitudes in the valley of decision. For "The Day of The Lord' is near in the valley of decision. 18 And it shall come to pass in 'That Day' that the mountains shall drip with new wine, the hills shall flow with milk, and all the brooks of Judah shall be flooded with water; a fountain shall flow from The House of The Lord and water The Valley of Acacias. Revelation 22:2: In the middle of its street, and on either side of 'The River,' was The Tree of Life, which bore twelve fruits, each tree yielding its fruit every month, The leaves of 'The Tree' were for 'The Healing of The Nations.'

Ezekiel 33:30: "As for you, son of man, the children of your people are talking about you beside the wall and in the doors of the houses; and they speak to one another, everyone saying to his brother, 'Please come and hear what 'The Word is that comes from The Lord,' 31 So they came to You as people do, they sit before You as My People, and they hear Your Words, but they do not do them; for with their mouth they show much love, but their hearts pursue their own gain. 32 "Indeed you are to them as a very lovely song of one who has a pleasant voice and can play well on an instrument; for they hear Your Words. but they do not do them." 33:33: "And when this comes to pass—surely it will come—then they will know that a prophet has been among them.

Ezekiel 35:1: Moreover The Word of The Lord came to me saying, 4 I shall lay your cities waste, and you shall be desolate. Then you shall know that I am The Lord. 5 Because you have had an ancient hatred, and have shed the blood of The Children of Israel by the power of The Sword at the time of their calamity, when their iniquity came to an end, 9 "See I will make you 'Perpetually desolate,' and your cities shall be uninhabited, then you shall know that I AM The Lord." 13 "Thus with your mouth you have boasted against Me and multiplied your words against Me; I have heard them."

36:2: 'Thus says The Lord God: "Because the enemy has said of you, Aha! The ancient heights have become our possession,'" 4 Therefore O Mountains of Israel, hear The Word of The Lord God! Thus says The Lord God to the mountains, the hills, the rivers, the valleys, the desolate wastes, and the cities that have been forsaken, which became plunder and mockery to the rest of the nations all around—8 "But you, O Mountains of Israel, you shall shoot forth your branches and yield your fruit to My People Israel, for they are about to come."

9 "For indeed I am for you, and I will turn you, and you shall be tilled and sown." 10 "I will multiply men upon you, all The House of Israel, all of it; and the cities shall be inhabited, and the ruins rebuilt. 11 "I will multiply upon you man and beast; and they shall increase and bear young; I will make you inhabited as in former times and do better for you than at your beginning. Then you shall know that I AM The Lord."

15 "Nor will I let you hear the taunts of the nation's anymore, nor bear the reproach of the peoples anymore, nor shall you cause your nation to stumble anymore, says The Lord God.'" 24 "For I will take you from among the nations, gather you out of all the countries, and bring you into your own land." 25 "Then I will sprinkle "Clean Water' on you and you shall be clean; I will cleanse you from all your filthiness and from all your idols." 26 "I will give you a 'New Heart' and put a 'New Spirit' within you, I will take the heart of stone out of your flesh and give you a heart of flesh." 27 "I will put 'My Spirit' within you and cause you to walk in 'My Statutes,' and you will keep 'My Judgments' and do them."

35 "So they will say, 'This land that was desolate has become like 'The Garden of Eden'; and the wasted, desolate, and ruined cities are now fortified and inhabited.' Ezekiel 39:28: 'Then they shall know that I Am The Lord their God, who sent them into captivity among the nations, but also brought them back to their land, and left none of them captive any longer. 29 'And I will not hide My Face from them anymore; for I shall have poured out 'My Spirit' on The House of Israel,' says The Lord God."

Psalms 107:28: Then they cry out to The Lord in their trouble, and He brings them out of their distresses. 30 Then they are glad because they are quiet; so, He guides then to their Desired Haven. 31 Oh, that men would give thanks to The Lord for His goodness, and for His wonderful works to The Children of Men! 35 He turns a wilderness into pools of water, and dry land into water springs. 42 The righteous see it and rejoice, and all iniquity stops its mouth. 43 Whoever is wise will observe these things, and they will understand 'The Lovingkindness of The Lord.'

Matthew 11:2: And when John had heard in prison about 'The Works of Christ,' he sent two of his disciples. 3 And said to Him, "Are You the 'Coming One,' or do we look for another? 4 Jesus answered and said to them, "Go and tell John the thing which you hear and see: 5 "The blind see and the lame walk; the leapers are cleansed and the deaf hear; the dead are raised up and the poor have the gospel preached to them." 6 "And blessed is he who is not offended because of Me."

19 "The son of man came eating and drinking, and they say, 'Look, a glutton and a winebibber, a friend of tax collectors and sinners!' But wisdom is justified by her children. 20 Then He begun to rebuke the cities in which most of His mighty works had been done, because they did not repent; 24 "But I say to you that it shall be more tolerable for the land of Sodom in The Day of Judgment than for you."

Matthew 12:26: "If Satan cast out Satan, he is divided against himself, how then will his kingdom stand?" 28 "But if I cast out demons by 'The Spirit of God,' surely 'The Kingdom of God' has come upon you." 36 "But I say to you that every idle word men may speak, they will give account of it in 'The Day of Judgment.'" 37 "For by your words you will be justified, and by your words you will be condemned."

Matthew 13:16: "But blessed are your eyes for they see, and your ears for they hear; 17 For Assuredly, I say to you that many prophets and righteous men desire to see what you see, and did not see it, and to hear what you hear, and did not hear it." 49 "So it will be at 'The End of The Age.' The angels will come forth, separate the wicked from among the just, 50 And cast them into the furnace of fire. There will be wailing and gnashing of teeth.

Isaiah 24:10: The city of confusion is broken down; every house is shut up so that none may go in. 12 In the city desolation is left, and the gate is stricken with destruction. 17 Fear and 'the pit' and the snare are upon you, O inhabitants of the earth. 18 And it shall be that he who flees from the noise of the fear shall fall into 'the pit,' and he who comes up from the midst of 'the pit' shall be caught in the snare; for the windows from on high are open, and the foundations of the earth are shaken. 19 The earth is violently broken, the earth is split open, the earth is shaken exceedingly.

21 It shall come to pass in 'That Day' that The Lord will punish on high the host of the exalted ones, and on the earth the kings of the earth. 22 They will be gathered together, as prisoners are gathered in the pit, and will be shut up in the prison; after many days they will be punished. 25:7: And He will destroy on this mountain the surface of the covering cast over all people, and the veil that is spread over all nations. 26:5: "For He brings down those who dwell on high, the lofty city; He lays it low; He lays it low to the ground, He brings it down to the dust. 6 The foot shall tread it down—the feet of the poor and the steps of the needy."

Isaiah 26:9: With My Soul I have desired you in the night, yes, by 'My Spirit' within Me 'I will seek you early'; for when Your Judgments are in the earth, the inhabitant of the world will learn righteousness. 10 Let grace be shown to the wicked, yet he will not learn righteousness; in The Land of Uprightness, he will deal unjustly and will not behold The Majesty of The Lord. 11 Lord, when Your Hand is lifted up, they will not see. But they will see and be ashamed for their envy of people; yes, the fire of Your enemies shall devour them.

13 O Lord our God, master's besides You have had dominion over us; but by You only we make mention of 'Your Name.' 14 They are dead, they will not live; they are deceased, they will not rise. Therefore, You have punished and destroyed them and made all their memory to perish. 18 We have been with child, we have been in pain; we have, as

it were, brought forth wind; we have not accomplished any deliverance in the earth, nor have the inhabitants of the world fallen.

21 For behold, The Lord comes out of His place to punish the inhabitants of the earth for their iniquity; the earth will also disclose her blood, and no more cover her slain. 27:1: In 'That Day' The Lord with His severe sword, great and strong, will punish Leviathan the fleeing serpent, Leviathan that twisted serpent; and He will slay the reptile that is in sea. Ezekiel 27:26: "Your oarsmen brought you into many waters, but the east wind broke you in the midst of the sea. 27 "Your riches, wares, and merchandise, your mariners and pilots, your caulkers and merchandisers, all your men of war who are in you and the entire company, which is in your midst, will fall into the midst of the seas on The Day of your ruin."

Ezekiel 28:2: "Son of man, say to the prince of Tyre, 'Thus says The Lord God: Because your heart is lifted up, and you say: 'I am a god, I set in the seat of gods, in the midst of the sea, yet you are a man and not a god, though you set your heart as the heart of god. 3 (Behold, you are wiser than Daniel! There is no secret that can be hidden from you! 4 With your wisdom and your understanding you have gained riches for yourselves, and gathered gold and silver into your treasures; 5 By your great wisdom in trade you have increased your riches, and your heart is lifted up because of your riches)."

7 Behold therefore, I will bring strangers against you, the most terrible of the nations; and they shall draw their swords against the beauty of your wisdom and defile your splendor. 8 They shall throw you down into 'the pit,' and you shall die the death of the slain in the midst of the seas. 9 "Will you still say before him who slays you, 'I am a god'? But you shall be a man, and not a god, in the hand of him who slays you. 10 You shall die the death of the uncircumcised by the hand of aliens; for I have spoken," says The Lord God.'"

Ezekiel 28:13: You were in Eden, 'The Garden of God'; every precious stone was your covering; the sardius, topaz, and diamond, beryl, onyx, and jasper, sapphire, turquoise, and emerald with gold. The workmanship of your timbrels and pipes was prepared for you on the day you were created. 14 "You were the anointed cherub who cover; I established you; you were on 'The Holy Mountain of God'; you walked back and forth in the midst of fiery stones." 15 You were perfect in your ways from the day you were created, till iniquity was found in you. 16 "By the abundance of your trading you became filled with violence within, and you sinned; therefore, I cast you as a profane thing out of The Mountain of God; and I destroyed you, O covering cherub, from the midst of the fiery stones."

17 "Your heart was lifted up because of your beauty; you corrupted your wisdom for the sake of your splendor, I cast you to the ground, I laid you before kings, that they might gaze at you." 18 "You defiled your sanctuaries by the multitude of your iniquities, by the iniquity of your trading; therefore I brought fire from your midst; it devoured you, and I turned you to ashes upon the earth in the sight of all who saw you." 19 All who knew you among the peoples are astonished at you; you have become a horror, and shall be no more forever.'"

Revelation 20:10: The devil, who deceived them, was cast into the lake of fire and brimstone, where the beast and the false prophets are. And they will be tormented day and night forever and ever. 12 And I saw the dead, small and great, standing before God; and books were opened. And another book was opened, which is 'The Book of Life,' and the dead were judged according to their works, by the things which were written in the books. 13 The sea gave up the dead who were in it, and death and hades delivered up the dead who were in them. And they were judged, each one according to his works. 14 Then death and hades were cast in the lake of fire. This is the second death. 15 And anyone not found written in 'The Book of Life' was cast into the lake of fire.

Revelation 21:1: Now I saw a 'New Heaven' and a 'New Earth,' for the first heaven and the first earth had passed away. Also there was no more sea. 6 And He said to Me, "It is done! I am The Alpha and The Omega, The Beginning and The End. I will give of The Fountain of The Water of Life freely to him who thirsts." 7 "He who overcomes shall inherit all things, and I will be his God and he shall be My son. 8 "But the cowardly, unbelieving, abominable, murderers, sexually immoral, sorcerers, idolaters, and all liars shall have their part in the lake which burns with fire and brimstone, which is the second death."

Ezekiel 28:20: Then 'The Word of The Lord' came to me, saying, 21 "Son of man, set your face toward Sidon, and prophesy against her; 22 And say, 'Thus says The Lord God: "Behold, I am against you, O Sidon; I will be glorified in your midst; and they shall know that I am

The Lord, when I execute judgments in her and am hallowed in her. 23 For I will send pestilence upon her, and blood in her streets; the wounded shall be judged in her midst by 'The Sword' against her on every side; Then they shall know that I am The Lord. 25 "Thus says The Lord God: "When I have gathered The House of Israel from the peoples among whom they are scattered, and am hallowed in them in the sight of the Gentiles, then they will dwell in their own land which I gave to My servant Jacob."

Nehemiah 1:8: "Remember, I pray, The Word that You commanded Your servant Moses, saying, 'If you are unfaithful,' I will scatter you among the nations, 6 But if you return to Me, and keep My commandments and 'do them,' though some of you were cast out to the farthest part of the heavens, yet I will gather them from there, and bring them to the place which I have chosen as 'A Dwelling Place For My Name.'" 10 Now these are Your servants and 'Your People,' whom You have Redeemed by Your great power, and by Your strong hand. 11 "O Lord, I pray, please let Your ear be attentive to the prayer of Your servant, and to the prayer of Your servants who desire to 'Fear Your Name'; and let Your servant prosper this day, I pray, and grant him mercy in the sight of this man.' For I was the king's cupbearer."

Job 10:1: 'My soul loathes my life; I will give free course to my complaint; I will speak in the bitterness of my soul. 2 I will say to God, 'Do not condemn me, show me why You contend with me. 3 Does it seem good to You that You should oppress, that You should despise 'The Work of Your Hands,' and smile on the counsel of the wicked? 4 Do You have eyes of flesh? Or do You see as man sees? 5 Are 'Your Days' like the days of mortal man? Are 'Your Years' like the days of a mighty man? 6 That You should seek for my iniquity and search out my sin, 7 Although You know that I am not wicked, and there is no one who can deliver from 'Your Hand'?

Psalms 97:1: The Lord Reigns; let the earth rejoice; let the multitude of isles be glad! 2 Clouds and darkness surround Him, righteousness and justice are the foundation of His throne. 3 A fire goes before Him and burns up His enemies round about. 4 His lightnings light the world; the earth sees and trembles. 5 The mountains melt like wax at 'The Presence of The Lord' of the whole earth. 10 You who love The Lord, hate evil! He preserves the souls of 'His Saint'; He delivers them out of the hand of the wicked.

Malachi 2:1: "And now, O priests, this commandment is for you. 2 If you will not hear, and if you will not take it to heart, to give glory to 'My Name,'" says The Lord of hosts, "I will send a curse upon you, and I will curse your blessings. Yes, I have cursed them already, because you did not take it to heart." 3 "Behold, I will rebuke your descendants and spread refuse on your face, the refuse of your solemn feasts; and 'One' will take you away with it. 4 Then you shall know that I have sent this commandment to you, that My Covenant with Levi may continue," says The Lord of hosts. 5 My Covenant was with him, one of life and peace, and I gave them to him that he might fear Me; so, he feared Me and was reverent before MY Name. 6 'The Law of Truth' was in his mouth, and injustice was not found on his lips. He walked with Me in peace and equity and turned many from iniquity. 7 "For the lips of a priest should keep knowledge, and people should seek 'The Law' from his mouth; for he is the messenger of The Lord of hosts." 8 But you have departed from the way; you have cause many to stumble at 'The Law.' You have corrupted The Covenant of Levi," says The Lord of hosts.

9 Therefore I also have made you contemptible and base before all the people, because you have shown partiality in 'The Law," 10 Have we not all 'One Father'? Has not 'One God created us? Why do we deal treacherously with one another by profaning The Covenant of the fathers? 17 You have wearied The Lord with your words; yet you say, "In what way have we wearied Him? In that you say, "Everyone who does evil is good in The Sight of The Lord, and He delights in them," or "Where is The God of Justice?"

3:13: "Your words have been harsh against Me," says The Lord. "Yet you say, 'What have we spoken against You? 14 You have said, 'It is useless to serve God; what profit is it that we have kept His ordinance, and that we have walked as mourners before The Lord of hosts?' 15 So now we call the proud blessed, for those who do wickedness are raised up; they even tempt God and go free."

I Peter 2:11: Behold, I beg you as sojourners and pilgrims, abstain from fleshly lusts which war against the soul. 12 Having your conduct honorable among the Gentiles, that when they speak against you as evildoers, they may, by your good works which they observe, glorify God in 'The Day of Visitation.' 15 For this is 'The Will of God,' that by doing good you may put to silence the ignorance of foolish men—

16 As free, yet not using liberty as a cloak for vise, but as bondservants of God. 25 For you were like sheep going astray but have now returned to 'The Shepherd and Overseer of your soul.'

3:12: For The Eyes of The Lord are on the righteous, and His ears are opened to their prayers; but The Face of The Lord is against those who do evil. 13 And who is he who will harm you if you become followers of what is good? 14 But even if you should suffer for righteousness' sake, you are blessed. "And do not be afraid of their threats, nor be troubled." 17 For it is better, if it is 'The Will of God,' to suffer for doing good than doing evil.

4:3: For we have spent enough of our past lifetime in doing the will of the Gentiles—when we walked in lewdness, lusts, drunkenness, revelries, drinking parties, and abominable idolatries. 4 In regard to these, they think it strange that you do not run with them in the same flood of dissipation, speaking evil of you. 5 They will give an account to Him who is ready to judge the living and the dead. 12 Beloved, do not think it strange concerning 'The Fiery Trial' which is to try you, as though some strange thing happened to you; 13 But rejoice to the extent that you partake of Christ's sufferings, that when His Glory is revealed, you may also be glad with exceeding joy. 14 If you are reproached for The Name of Christ, blessed are you, for 'The Spirit of Glory' and of God rests upon you. On their part He is blasphemed, but on your part 'He is Glorified.' 15 But let none of you suffer as a murderer, a thief, and evildoer, or as a busybody in other people's matters. 16 Yet if anyone suffers as 'A Christian, let him not be ashamed, but let him Glorify God in this matter. 17 For 'The Time' has come for judgment to begin at 'The House of God'; and if it begins with us first, what will be the end of those who do not obey 'The Gospel of God'?

I Peter 5:6: Therefore humble yourselves under 'The Mighty Hand of God,' that He may exalt you in due time. 7 Casting all your cares upon Him, for He cares for you. 8 Be sober, be vigilant; because your adversary the devil walks about like a roaring lion, seeking whom he may devour. 9 Resist him, steadfast in the faith, knowing that the same sufferings are experienced by your brotherhood in the world.

II Peter 1:12: For this reason I will not be negligent to remind you always of these things, though you know and are established in the present truth. 16 For we did not follow cunningly devised fables when we made known to you 'The Power and Coming of our Lord Jesus Christ,' but were eyewitnesses of 'His Majesty.' 17 For He received from God The Father honor and glory when such 'A Voice' came to Him from 'The Excellent Glory': "This is My Beloved Son, in whom I am well pleased." 18 And we heard 'This Voice' which came from heaven when we were with Him on The Holy Mountain.

19 And so we have 'The Prophetic Word' confirmed, which you do well to heed as a light that shines in a dark place, until the day dawns and the morning star rises in your hearts: 20 Knowing this first, that no prophecy of scripture is of any private interpretation. 21 For prophesy never came by the will of man, but Holy Men of God spoke as they were moved by The Holy Spirit.

2:1: But there were also false prophets among the people, even as there will be false teachers among you, who will secretly bring in destructive heresies, even denying The Lord who brought them, and bring on themselves swift destruction. 2 And many will follow their destructive ways, because of who 'The Way of Truth' will be blasphemed. 3 By covetousness they will exploit you with deceptive words; for a long time 'The Judgment' has not been idle, and the destruction does not slumber. 4 For if God did not spare the angels who sinned but cast them down to hell and delivered them to chains of darkness, to be reserved for judgment.

8 (For that righteous man, dwelling among them, tormented his righteous soul from day to day by seeing and hearing their lawless deeds)—9 Then The Lord knows how to deliver the godly out of temptations and to reserve the unjust under punishment for 'The Day of Judgment.' 10 And especially those who walk according to the flesh in the lust of uncleanness and despise authority. They are presumptuous self-willed. They are not afraid to speak evil of dignitaries. 12 But these, like natural brute beasts made to be caught and destroyed, speak evil of the things they do not understand, and will utterly perish their own corruption. 13 And will receive 'the wages of unrighteousness,' as those who count it pleasure to carouse in the daytime. They are spots and blemishes, carousing in their own deceptions while they feast with you.

14 Having eyes full of adultery and that cannot cease from sin, enticing unstable souls. They have a heart trained in covetous practices and are accursed children. 15 They have forsaken 'The Right Way' and

gone astray, following the way of Balaam the son of Beor, who loved the wages of unrighteousness. 17 These are wells without water, clouds carried by a tempest, for whom is reserved the blackness of darkness forever. 18 For when they speak great swelling words of emptiness, they allure through the lusts of the flesh, through lewdness, the ones who have escaped from those who live in error.

Ecclesiastes 4:1: Then I returned and considered all the oppression that is done under the sun; and look! The tears of the oppressed, but they had no comforter; on the side of their oppressors there is power, but they had no comforter. 2 Therefore I praised the dead who were already dead more than the living who are still alive. 3 Yet, better then both is he who has never existed, who has not seen the evil work that is done under the sun.

5:2: Do not be rash with your mouth and let not your heart utter anything hastily before God. For God is in heaven, and you on earth; therefore, let your words be few. 6 Do not let your mouth cause your flesh to sin, nor say before 'The Messenger of God' that it was an error. Why should God be angry at your excuse and destroy the works of your hands. 6:7: All the labor of man is for his mouth, and yet the soul is not satisfied.

7:25: I applied my heart to know, to search and seek out wisdom and the reason of things, to know the wickedness of folly, even of foolishness and madness. 8:17: Then I saw all 'The Works of God,' that a man cannot find out the work that is done under the sun. For though a man labors to discover it, yet he will not find it; moreover, though a wise man attempts to know it, he will not be able to find it. 9:3: This is an evil in all that is done under the sun: that one thing happens to all. Truly the hearts of the sons of man are full of evil; madness is in their hearts while they live, and after that they go to the dead.

5 For the living know that they will die; but the dead know nothing, and they have no more reward, for the memory of them is forgotten. 6 Also their love, their hatred, and their envy have now perished; nevermore will they have a share in anything done under the sun. 10 Whatever your hand finds to do, do it with all your might; for there is no work or devise or knowledge or wisdom in the grave where you are going.

11:5: As you do not know what is the way of the wind, or how the bones grow in the womb of her who is with child, so you do not know 'The Works of God' who makes everything. 12:9: And moreover, because the preacher was wise, he still taught the people knowledge; Yes, he pondered and sought out and set in order many proverbs. 10 The preacher sought to find acceptable words' and what was written was Upright—'Words of Truth.'

1 Timothy 1:9: Knowing this: that 'The Law' is not made for the righteous person but for the lawless and insubordinate, for the ungodly and for sinners, for the unholy and profane, for murderers of fathers and murderers of mothers, for manslayers. 10 For fornicators, for sodomites, for kidnappers, for liars, for perjures, and if there is any other thing that is contrary to 'Sound Doctrine.' 11 According to 'The Glorious Gospel of The Blessed God, which was committed to my trust. I Chronicles 28:19 "All This," said David, "The Lord made me understand in writing, by 'His Hand Upon Me,' all 'The Works of These Plans.'"

Isaiah 8:18: Here am I and The Children who The Lord has given Me! We are for signs and wonders in Israel from The Lord of hosts, who dwells in Mount Zion. 19 And when they say to you, "Seek, those who are mediums and wizards, who whisper and mutter," Should not a people seek their God? Should they seek the dead-on behalf of the living? To 'The Law' and to 'The Testimony'! If they do not speak according to 'This Word,' it is because there is no light in them.

9:2: The people who walked in darkness have seen 'A Great Light'; those who dwelt in 'The Land of The Shadow of Death,' upon them 'A Light' has shined. 13 For the people do not turn to Him who strikes them, nor do they seek The Lord of hosts. 14 Therefore The Lord will cut off head and tail from Israel, palm branch and bulrush in one day. 15 The elder and honorable, he is the head; the prophet who teaches lies, he is the tail. 16 For the leaders of this people cause then to err, and those who are led by them are destroyed. 17 Therefore The Lord will have no joy in their young men, nor have mercy of their fatherless and widows: for everyone is a hypocrite and an evildoer, and every mouth speaks folly. For all this His anger is not turned away, but His Hand is stretched out still.

Isaiah 10:20: And it shall come to pass in That Day that the remnant of Israel, and such as have escaped of The House of Jacob, will never again depend on him who defeated them, but will depend on The Lord, The Holy One of Israel, in "TRUTH." Isaiah 11:1: There shall come forth 'A Rod' from The Stem of Jesse, and 'A Branch' shall grow out of his roots. 2 'The Spirit of The Lord' shall rest upon Him, 'The Spirit of Wisdom and Understanding,' 'The Spirit of Counsel and Might,' 'The Spirit of Knowledge and of The Fear of The Lord.'

3 His delight is in 'The Fear of The Lord,' and He shall not judge by the sight of His eyes, nor decide by the hearing of His ears: 4 But with righteousness He shall judge the poor and decide with equity for the meek of the earth; He shall strike the earth with 'The Rod of His Mouth,' and with 'The Breath of His Lips' He shall slay the wicked. 5 Righteousness shall be the belt of His loins, and faithfulness the belt of His waist.

6 "The wolf also shall dwell with the lamb, the leopard shall lie down with the young goat, the calf and the young lion and the fatling together; and a little child shall lead them. 7 The cow and the bear shall graze; their young ones shall lie down together; and the lion shall eat straw like the ox. The nursing child shall play by the cobra's hole, and the weaned child shall put his hand in the viper's den. 9 They shall not hurt nor destroy in all 'My Holy Mountain,' for the earth shall be full of 'The Knowledge of The Lord' as the waters cover the sea.

10 "And in 'That Day' there shall be 'A Root of Jesse,' who shall stand as 'A Banner' to the people; for the Gentiles shall seek Him, and 'His Resting Place' shall be glories. 11 It shall come to pass in 'That Day' that The Lord shall set 'His Hand' again 'The Second Time' to recover the remnant of His People who are left, from Assyria and Egypt, from Pathros and Cush, from Elam and Shinar, from Hamath and the islands of the sea. 15 The Lord will utterly destroy the tongue of the Sea of Egypt; with 'His Mighty Wind' He will shake His fist over the river, and strike it in the seven streams, and make men cross over dry-shod.

Isaiah 12:1: "And in 'That Day' you will say: "O Lord, I will praise You thought You were angry with me, Your anger is turned away, and You comfort me." 2 Behold, God is my Salvation, I will trust and not be afraid; 'For YAH, The Lord, is my strength and song; He also has become my Salvation,'" 6 Cry out and shout, O inhabitants of Zion, for 'Great' is The Holy One of Israel in your midst.

Isaiah 13:3: "I have commanded 'My Sanctified Ones'; I have also called 'My Mighty Ones'; for My anger—those who rejoice in 'My

Exaltation.'" 4 The noise of a multitude in the mountains, like that of many people! A tumultuous noise of the kingdoms of nations gathered together! The Lord of hosts musters the army for battle. 5 They come from a far country, from the end of heaven—The Lord and His weapons of indignation, to destroy the whole land. 6 Wail, for 'The Day of The Lord' is "At Hand"! I will come as destruction from 'The Almighty.' 9 Behold 'The Day of The Lord' comes, cruel, with both wrath and fierce anger, to lay the land desolate; and He will destroy its sinners from it.

10 For the stars of heaven and their constellations will not give their light; the sun will be darkened in its going forth, and the moon will not cause its light to shine. 11 "I will punish the world for its evil, and the wicked for their iniquity; I will halt the arrogance of the proud and will lay low the haughtiness of the terrible. 13 Therefore I will shake the heavens, and the earth will move out of her place, in 'The Wrath of The Lord of Hosts' and in 'The Day' of His Fierce Anger.

II Chronicles 7:13: "When I shut up heaven and there is no rain, or command the locusts to devour the land, or send pestilence among the people, 14 If My People who are called by 'My Name' will humble themselves, and pray and seek My Face, and turn from their wicked ways, then I will hear from heaven, and will forgive their sin and heal their land." 19 "But if you turn away and forsake My statutes and My commandments which I have set before you, and go and serve other gods, and worship them, 20 Then I will uproot them from 'My Land' which I have given them, and this house which I sanctified for My Name I will cast out of 'My Sight,' and will make it a proverb and a byword among all peoples. Romans 3:18: "There is no fear of God before their eyes."

Romans 3:19: Now we know that whatever 'The Law' says, it says to those who are under 'The Law,' that every mouth may be stopped, and all the world may become guilty before God. 23 For all have sinned and fall short of 'The Glory of God.' Romans 8:6: For to be carnally minded is death, but to be 'Spiritually Minded' is 'Life and Peace.' 27 Now He who searches the heart knows the mind of 'The Spirit' is, because He makes intercession for the saints according to 'The Will of God.' 29 For whom He foreknew, He also predestined to be conformed to the image of His Son, that He might be the firstborn among many brethren.

Romans 8:31: What then shall we say to these things? If God is for us, who can be against us? 33 Who shall bring 'A Charge' against God's Elect? It is God who justifies. 35 Who shall separate us from 'The Love of Christ'? Shall tribulation, or distress, or persecution, or famine, or nakedness, or peril, or sword? 9:1: I tell you 'The Truth' in Christ, I am not lying, my conscience also bearing me witness in 'The Holy Spirit.' 6 But it is not that 'The Word of God, has taken no effect. For they are not all Israel who are of Israel.

Revelation 3:9: "Indeed I will make those of The Synagogue of Satan, who say they are Jews and are not, but lie—indeed I will make them come and worship before your feet, and to know that I have loved you." 10 "Because you have kept 'My Command' to preserve, I also will keep you from 'The Hour of Trial' which shall come upon the whole world, to test those who dwell on the earth." 15 "I know your works, that you are neither cold nor hot. I could wish you were cold or hot." 10 So then, because you are lukewarm, and neither cold nor hot, I will vomit you out of My Mouth. 17 "Because you say, 'I am rich, have become wealthy, and have need of nothing'—and do not know that you are wretched, miserable, poor, blind, and naked—19 "As many as I love, I rebuke and chasten, therefore be zealous and repent.

Psalms 89:19: Then You spoke in 'A Vision' to Your Holy One and said: "I have given help to 'One' who is mighty; I have exalted 'One Chosen' from the people. 20 I have found My servant David; with My Holy Oil I have anointed Him, 21 With whom My Hand shall be established; also, My Arm shall strengthen Him.

Luke 24:38: And He said to them, "Why are you troubled? And why do doubts arise in your hearts? 39 "Behold My hands and My feet, that it is I Myself. Handle Me and see, for 'A Spirit' does not have flesh and bones as you see I have." John 1:1: In the beginning was 'The Word,' and 'The Word' was with God, and 'The Word' was God. 14 And 'The Word' became flesh and dwelt among us, and we beheld 'His Glory,' The Glory as of 'The Only Begotten of The Father,' full of grace and Truth.

John 3:12: "If I have told you earthly things and you do not believe, how will you believe if I tell you heavenly things?" 17 "For God did not send His Son into the world to condemn the world, but that the world through Him might be saved." 19 "And this is the condemnation, that

'The Light' has come into the world, and men love darkness rather than light, because their deeds were evil." 20 "For everyone practicing evil hates 'The Light' and does not come to 'The Light,' lest his deeds should be exposed."

John 5:45: "Do not think that I shall accuse you to 'The Father,' there is one who accuses you—Moses, in whom you trust." 46 "For if you believe Moses, you will believe Me; for he wrote about Me." 47 "But if you do not believe his writings, how will you believe 'My Words'?"

John 7:16: Jesus answered them and said, "My Doctrine is not Mine, but His who sent Me." 17 "If anyone wills to do His will, he shall know concerning the doctrine, whether it is from God or whether I speak on My own authority. II Corinthians 13:5: Examine yourselves as whether you are in the faith. Test yourselves. Do you not know yourselves, that Jesus Christ is in you?—Unless indeed you are disqualified. 6 But I trust that you will know that we are not disqualified. 8 For we can do nothing against 'The Truth,' but for 'The Truth.' 10 Therefore I write these things being absent, lest being present I should use sharpness, according to the authority which The Lord has given to Me for edification and not for destruction.

Galatians 1:6: I marvel that you are turning away so soon from Him who called you in the grace of Christ, to a different gospel. 7 Which is not another; but there are some who trouble you and want to pervert 'The Gospel of Christ. 8 But even if we, or an angel from heaven, preach any other gospel to you then what we have preached to you, let him be accursed. 10 For do I now persuade man, or God? Or do I seek to please men? For if I still please men, I would not be a bondservant of Christ.

11 But I make known to you, brethren, that 'The Gospel' which was preached by Me is not according to man. 12 For I neither received it from man, nor was I taught it, but it came through 'The Revelation of Jesus Christ.' 20 (Now concerning the things which I write to you, indeed, before God, I do not lie.) Galatians 2:4 And this occurred because of false brethren secretly brought in. (Who came in by stealth to spy out our liberty which we have in Christ Jesus, that they might bring us into bondage), 5 To whom we did not yield submission even for an hour, that 'The Truth' of 'The Gospel' might continue with us.

Galatians 2:6: But from those who seem to be something—whatever they were, it makes no difference to Me; God shows personal favoritism to no man—for those who seemed to be something added nothing to Me. 6:3: For if anyone thinks himself to be something, when he is nothing, he deceives himself. 7 Do not de deceived, God is not mocked; for whatever a man sows, that he will also reap.

Micah 6:1: Hear now what The Lord says: "Arise, plead your case before the mountains and let the hills hear your voice. 2 Hear, O your mountains, 'The Lord's Complaint,' and you strong foundations of the earth; for The Lord has a complaint against His people, and He will contend with Israel. 9 The Lord's Voice cries to the city—wisdom shall see 'Your Name': "Hear The Rod! Who has appointed it?"

12 For her rich men are full of violence, her inhabitants have spoken lies, and their tongue is deceitful in their mouth. 7:3 That they may successfully do evil with both hands—the prince asks for gifts, the judge seek a bribe, and the great men utters his evil desire; so they scheme together. 4 The best of them is like a brier; the most upright is sharper than a thorn hedge; 'The Day' of your watchman and your punishment comes; now shall be their perplexity.

Job 11:5: But oh, that God would speak, and open His lips against you. 6 That He would show you 'The Secrets of Wisdom'! For they would double your prudence, know therefore that God exacts from you less than your iniquity deserves. 7 "Can you search out 'The Deep Things of God'? Can you find out the limits of The Almighty? 8 They are higher than heaven—what can you do? Deeper than Shoel—what can you know? 10 "If He passes by, imprisons, and gathers to judgment, then who can hinder Him?"

13 "If you would prepare your heart, and stretch out your hands toward Him;" 14 If iniquity were in your hand, and you put it far away, and would not let wickedness dwell in your tents; 15 Then surely you could lift up your face without spot; yes, you could be steadfast, and not fear: 16 Because you would forget your misery, and remember it as waters that have passed away, 17 And your life would be brighter than noonday, Though you were dark, you would be like the morning. 18 And you would be secure, because there is hope, yes, you would dig around you, and take your rest in safety. 20 But the eyes of the wicked will fail, and they shall not escape, and their hope—loss of life!"

Isaiah 5:13: Therefore My people have gone into captivity, because they have no knowledge; their honorable men are famished, and their multitude dried up with thirst, 14 Therefore Shoel has enlarged itself and open its mouth beyond measure; their glory and their multitude and their pomp, and he who is jubilant, shall descend into it. 15 People shall be brought down, each man shall be humbled, and the eyes of the lofty shall be humbled.

23 Who justify the wicked for a bribe and take away justice from the righteous man! 24 Therefore, as the fire devours the stubble, and the flame consumes the chaff, so their root will be rottenness, and their blossom will ascend like dust; because they have rejected 'The Law of The Lord of hosts,' and despised 'The Word' of The Holy One of Israel. 25 Therefore The Anger of The Lord is aroused against His people; He has stretched out His Hand against them and stricken them, and the hills trembled. Their carcasses were as refuse in the midst of the streets. For all this His anger is not turning away, but His Hand is stretched out still.

Isaiah 6:8: Also I heard 'The Voice of The Lord,' saying: "Whom shall I send, and who will go for us?" Then I said, "Here I Am! Send Me." 9 And He said, "Go, and tell this people: Keep on hearing, but do not understand; keep on seeing, but do not perceive." 10 Make the heart of this people dull, and their ears heavy, and shut their eyes; lest they see with their eyes, and hear with their ears, and understand with their heart, and return and be healed. 11 Then I said, "Lord, how long?" And He answered: "Until the cities are laid waste and without inhabitants, the houses are without a man, the land is utterly desolate. 12 The Lord has removed men far away and the forsaken places are many in the midst of the land."

8:10: Take counsel together, but it will come to nothing; speak the word, but it will not stand, for God is with us. 11 For The Lord spoke thus to Me with a strong hand and instructed Me that I should not walk in the way of this people, saying: 12 "Do not say, 'A Conspiracy;' concerning all that this people call a conspiracy, nor be afraid of their threats, nor be troubled. 13 The Lord of hosts, Him shall you hallow; let Him be your fear and let Him be your dread. 14 He will be as a sanctuary, but a stone of stumbling and a rock of offense to both The House of Israel, as a trap and a snare to The Inhabitants of Jerusalem. 15 And many among them shall stumble; they shall fall and be broken, be snared and taken."

Jeremiah 7:17: "Do you not see what they do in the cities of Judah and in the streets of Jerusalem? 18 The children gather wood, the fathers kindle the fire, and the woman knead dough, to make cakes for the queen of heaven; they pour out drink offerings to other gods, that they may provoke Me to anger." 19 "Do they not provoke Me to anger?" says The Lord. "Do they not provoke themselves, to the shame of their own faces?"

28 "So you shall say this to them, 'This is a nation that does not obey 'The Voice of The Lord Their God' nor receives correction, 'Truth' has perished and has been cut off from their mouth. 33 The corpses of this people will be food for the birds of the heaven and for the beasts of the earth. And no one will frighten them away. 34 Then I will cause to cease from the cities of Judah and from the streets of Jerusalem the Voice of mirth and the Voice of gladness, The Voice of The Bridegroom and the Voice of the bride, For the land shall be desolate.

Jeremiah 8:8: "How can you say, 'We are wise, and The Law of The Lord is with us'? Look, the false pen of the scribe certainly works falsehood." Luke 11:42: "But woe to you Pharisees! For you tithe mint and rue and all manner of herbs and pass by 'Justice and The Love of God.' These you ought to have done, without leaving the others undone." 52 "Woe to you lawyers! For you have taken away 'The Key of Knowledge'. You did not enter in yourselves, and those who were entering in you hindered." Matthew 23:25: "Woe to you, scribes and Pharisees, hypocrites! For you cleanse the outside of the cup and dish, but inside they are full of extortion and self-indulgence.

28 "Even so you also outwardly appear righteous to men, but inside you are full of hypocrisy and lawlessness." 33 "Serpents, brood of vipers! How can you escape the condemnation of hell? 38 "See, your house is left to you desolate; 39 "For I say to you, you shall see Me no more till you say, 'Blessed is He who comes in The Name of The Lord!'" 25:26: "And at midnight a cry was heard: 'Behold, The Bridegroom is coming; go out to meet Him!'"

John 16:7: "Nevertheless I tell you "The Truth.' It is to your advantage that I go away; for if I do not go away, 'The Helper' will not come to you; but if I depart, I will send Him to you." 8 "And when He has come, He will convict the world of sin, and of righteousness, and of judgment: 9 "Of sin, because they do not believe in Me." 10 "Of righteousness, because I go to My Father and you see Me no more;" 11 "Of judgment, because the ruler of this world is judged."

John 16:13: "However, when He, 'The Spirit of Truth,' has come, He will guide you into 'All Truth'; for He will not speak on His own authority, but whatever He hears He will speak; and He will tell you things to come." 14 "He will 'Glorify Me,' for He will take of what is Mine and declare it to you."

Jeremiah 10:7: Who would not fear You, O King of the nations? For 'This' is 'Your Rightful Due,' for among all the wise men of the nations and in all the kingdoms, there is none like You. 8 But they are altogether dull-hearted and foolish, a wooden idol is a worthless doctrine. 10 But The Lord is 'The True God'; He is 'The Living God' and 'The Everlasting King.' At 'His Wrath' the earth will tremble, and the nations will not be able to endure 'His Indignation.'

Psalms 27:13: I would have lost heart, unless I had believed that I would see 'The Goodness of The Lord' in the land of the living. 28:13: Do not take me away with the wicked and with the workers of iniquity, who speak peace to their neighbors, but evil is in their hearts. 4 Give them according to their deeds, and according to the wickedness of their endeavors; give them according to the work of their hands; render to them what they deserve. 5 Because they do not regard 'The Works of The Lord,' nor 'The Operation of His Hands,' He shall destroy them and not build them up.

Philippians 2:13: For it is God who works in you both to will and to do for His good pleasure. 15 That you may become blameless, and harmless, Children of God without fault in the midst of a crooked and perverse generation among whom you 'shine as lights' in the world. 19 But I trust in The Lord Jesus to send Timothy to you shortly, that I also may be encouraged when I know of your state. 22 But you know His proven character, that as 'A Son' with His Father He served with me in 'The Gospel.' 28 Therefore I sent Him the more eagerly, that when you see Him again you may rejoice, and I may be less sorrowful. 30 Because for 'The Work of Christ' He came close to death, not regarding His life, to supply what was lacking in your service toward me.

I John 3:10: In 'This' The Children of God and the children of the devil are manifest: whoever does not practice righteousness is not of God, nor is he who does not love his brother. 12 Not as Cain who was of the wicked one and murdered his brother, And why did he murder him? Because his works were evil and his brothers righteous. II John 1:7: For many deceivers have gone out into the world who do not confess Jesus Christ as coming in the flesh. This is a deceiver and an anti-Christ. Jude 1:4: For certain men have crept in unnoticed, who long ago were marked out for this condemnation, ungodly men, who turn 'The Grace of Our God' into lewdness and deny 'The Only Lord God' and our Lord Jesus Christ.

5 But I want to remind you, though you once knew this, that The Lord, having saved the people out of the land of Egypt, afterward destroyed those who did not believe. 6 And the angels who did not keep their proper domain, but left their own abode, He has reserved in ever-lasting chains under darkness for 'The Judgment of The Great Day'; 7 As Sodom and Gomorrah, and the cities around them in similar manner to these, having given themselves over to sexual immorality and gone after strange flesh, are set forth as an example suffering the vengeance of eternal fire.

8 Likewise also these dreamers defile the flesh, reject authority, and speak evil of dignitaries. 10 But these speak evil of whatever they do not know, and whatever they know naturally, like brute beasts, in these things they corrupt themselves. 11 Woe to them! For they have gone in the way of Cain, have run greedily in the error of Balaam for profit, and perished in the rebellion of Korah.

14 Now Enoch, the seventh from Adam, prophesied about these men also, saying, "Behold, The Lord comes with ten thousand of His Saints, 15 To execute judgment on all, to convict all who are ungodly among them of all their ungodly deeds which they have committed in an ungodly way. And of all the harsh things which ungodly sinners have spoken against Him," 16 These are grumblers, complainers, walking according to their own lusts: and they mouth great swelling words, flattering people to gain advantage, 19 These are sensual persons, who cause divisions, not having 'The Spirit.'

Haggai 2:3: "Who is left among you who saw this temple in its former glory? And how do you see it now? In comparison with it, is this not in your eyes nothing? 5 According to "The Word' that I covenanted with you when you came out of Egypt, so 'My Spirit' remains among you; do not fear. 9 The glory of this Latter Temple shall be greater than the former,' says The Lord of hosts. 'And in 'This Place' I will give peace, says The Lord of hosts.

Zechariah 1:2: "The Lord has been very angry with your fathers. 3 Therefore, say to them, 'Thus says The Lord of hosts: "Return to Me," says The Lord of hosts, "And I will return to you," says The Lord of hosts. 15 I am exceedingly angry with the nations at ease; for I was a little angry, and they helped—but with evil intent. 3:2: And The Lord said to Satan, "The Lord rebuke you, Satan! The Lord who has chosen Jerusalem rebuke you! Is this not a brand plucked from the fire?

5:3: Then He said to Me, "This is the curse that goes out over the face of the whole earth; 'every thief shall be expelled, according to this side of the scroll; and, every perjurer shall be expelled, according to that side of it." 4 "I will send out the curse," says The Lord of hosts; "It shall enter the house of the thief and the house of the one who swears falsely by My Name. It shall remain in the midst of his house and consume it, with its timber and stones.

8:9: Thus says The Lord of hosts: "Let your hands be strong, you who have been hearing in 'These Days' 'These Words' by the mouth of the prophets, who spoke in the day the foundation was laid for The House of The Lord of hosts, that the temple might be built. 10 For before these days there was no wages for man nor any hire for beast; there was no peace from the enemy for whoever went out or came in: for I set all men, everyone, against his neighbor." 14 "For thus says The Lord of hosts: 'Just as I determined to punish you when your fathers provoked Me to wrath,' says The Lord of hosts, 'And I would not relent,' 15 So again in 'These Days' I am determined to do Good to Jerusalem and to The House of Judah. Do Not Fear.

16 These are the things you shall do, speak each man 'The Truth' to his neighbor; give judgment in your gates for Truth, Justice, and Peace. 17 Let none of you think evil in your heart against your neighbor; and do not love a false oath. For all these things I hate; says The Lord."

9:9: "Rejoice greatly, O Daughter of Zion! Shout, O Daughter of Jerusalem! Behold, your King is coming to you; He is just and having salvation, lowly and riding on a donkey. 14:4: And in 'That Day' His feet will stand on The Mount of Olives, which faces Jerusalem on the east. And The Mount of Olives shall split in two, from east to west, making a very large valley; half of the mountain shall move toward the north and half of it toward the south.

Zechariah 14:5: Then you shall flee through My mountain valley, for the mountain valley shall reach to Azal. Yes, you shall flee as you fled from the earthquake in the days of Uzziah king of Judah. Thus The Lord My God will come, and all the saints with You. 6 It shall come to pass in 'That Day' there will be no light; the lights will diminish. 9 And The Lord shall be 'KING' over all the earth. In 'That Day' it shall be—"The Lord is One," and 'His Name One.'

12 And this is the plague with which The Lord will strike all the people who fought against Jerusalem: Their flesh shall dissolve while they stand on their feet, their eyes shall dissolve in their sockets, and their tongue shall dissolve in their mouths. 16 And it shall come to pass that everyone who is left of all the nations which come against Jerusalem from year to year to worship 'The King,' The Lord of hosts, and to keep The Feast of Tabernacles.

Psalms 102:15: So the nations shall fear The Name of The Lord, and all the kings of the earth Your Glory. 16 For The Lord shall build up Zion: He shall appear in His Glory. 18 This will be written for the generation to come, that a people 'Yet to be created' may praise The Lord. 25 Of old You laid the foundation of the earth, and the heavens are the works of Your hands. 26 They will perish, but you will endure: yes, they will grow old like a garment; like a cloak You will change them, and they will be changed.

Jeremiah 23:16: Thus says The Lord of hosts: "Do not listen to the words of the prophets who prophesy to you. They make you worthless; they speak a vision of their own heart, not from The Mouth of The Lord. 17 They continually say to those who despise Me, 'The Lord has said, "You shall have peace"; and to everyone who walks according to the dictates of his own heart, 'No evil shall come upon you,'" 18 For who has stood in 'The Counsel of The Lord,' and has perceived and heard 'His Word'? Who has marked 'His Word' and heard it?

22 But if they had stood in 'My Counsel' and had caused My People to hear 'My Words,' then they would have turned then from their evil way and from the evil of their doings. 25 "I have heard what the

prophets have said who prophesy lies in My Name, saying, 'I have dreamed, I have dreamed!" 27 "Who try to make My People forget My Name by their dreams which everyone tells his neighbor, as their fathers forgot My Name for Baal." 29 Is not 'My Word' like a fire? says The Lord, "And like a hammer that breaks the rock in pieces?

32 "Behold I am against those who prophesy false dreams," says The Lord, "and tell them, and cause My People to err by their lies and by their recklessness. Yet I did not send them or command them; therefore, they shall not profit this people at all," says The Lord. 34 "And as for the prophet and the priest and the people who say, 'The oracle of The Lord!' I will even punish that man and his house. 36 And the oracle of The Lord you shall mention no more, for every man's word will be his oracle, for you have perverted 'The Words of The Living God,' The Lord of hosts, our God. 40 'And I will bring an everlasting reproach upon you, and a perpetual shame which shall not be forgotten.'"

Jeremiah 25:7: "Yet you have not listened to Me," says The Lord, 'that you might provoke Me to anger with the works of your hands to your own hurt.'" 10 Moreover I will take from them the voice of mirth, and the voice of gladness, The Voice of The Bridegroom, and The Voice of The Bride, the sound of the millstones and the light of the lamp. 12 'Then it will come to pass when seventy years are completed, that I will punish the king of Babylon and that nation, the land of the Chaldeans, for their iniquity; says The Lord, and I will make it a perpetual desolation.'

26:3: 'Perhaps everyone will listen and turn from his evil way, that I may relent concerning the calamity which I purpose to bring on them because of the evil of their doings.' 13 "Now therefore, amend your ways and your doings, and obey The Voice of The Lord your God; then The Lord will relent concerning the doom that He has pronounced against you. 29:10: For thus says The Lord: after seventy years are completed at Babylon, I will visit you and perform 'My Good Word' toward you and cause you to return to 'This Place.'

11 For I know the thoughts that I think toward you, says The Lord, thoughts of peace and not of evil, to give you a future and a hope. 12 Then you will call upon Me and go and pray to Me, and I will listen to you. 13 And you will seek Me and find Me, when you search for Me

with your whole heart. 29:15 Because you have said, "The Lord has raised up prophets for us in Babylon'—

16 Therefore thus says The Lord concerning the king who sits on the throne of David, concerning all the people who dwell in this city, and concerning your brethren who have not gone out with you into captivity—17 Thus says The Lord of hosts: Behold, I will send on them 'The Sword,' the famine, and the pestilence, and make them like rotten figs that cannot be eaten, they are so bad. 18 And I will pursue them with 'The Sword, with famine, and with pestilence; and I will deliver them to trouble among all the kingdoms of the earth—to be a curse, an astonishment, a hissing, and a reproach among all the nations where I have driven them, 19 Because they have not heeded My Words, says The Lord, which I sent them by My servants the prophets rising up early and sending them; neither would you heed, says The Lord.

Psalms 99:2: The Lord is great in Zion, and He is high above all the peoples. 6 Moses and Aaron were among His priests, and Samuel was among those who called upon His Name; they call upon The Lord, and He answered them. 7 He spoke to them in the cloudy pillar; they kept His testimonies and the ordinance He gave them. Deuteronomy 11:20: "And you shall write them on your doorposts of your house and on the gates. 21 That your days and the days of your children may be multiplied in the land of which The Lord swore to your fathers to give them, like the days of the heavens above the earth.

24 "Every place on which the sole of your foot treads shall be yours: from the wilderness and Lebanon, from The River, the river Euphrates, even to the western sea, shall be your territory" 25 "No man shall be able to stand against you; The Lord your God will put the dread of you and the fear of you upon all the land where you tread, just as He has said to you.

26 "Behold, I set before you 'Today' a blessing and a curse." 27 "The blessing, if you obey the commandments of The Lord your God which I command you 'Today';" 28 "And a curse, if you do not obey the commandments of The Lord your God, but turn aside from 'The Way' which I command you 'Today,' to go after other gods which you have not known.

Psalms 2:2: The kings of the earth set themselves, and the rulers take counsel together, against The Lord and against 'His Anointed,' saying, 3 "Let us break their bonds in pieces and cast away their cords from us." 4 He who set in heaven shall laugh; The Lord shall hold them in derision. Now therefore, be wise, O kings, be instructed, you judge of the earth. 11 Serve The Lord with fear and rejoice with trembling.

Isaiah 34:5: "For 'My Sword' shall be bathed in heaven; indeed, it shall come down on Edom, and on the people of My curse, for judgment, 8 For it is 'The Day' of the Lord's vengeance, the year of recompense for 'The Cause of Zion.' 35:4: Say to those who are fearful-hearted, "Be strong, and do not fear! Behold, your God will come with vengeance, with the recompense of God: He will come and save you." 5 Then the eyes of the blind shall be opened, and the ears of the deaf shall be unstopped. 6 The lame shall leap like a deer, and the tongue of the dumb sing. For waters shall burst forth in the wilderness, and streams in the desert.

Isaiah 40:2: "Speak comfort to Jerusalem and cry out to her, that her warfare is ended, that her iniquity is pardoned; for she has received from The Lord's hand double for all her sins. 3 'The Voice' of 'One' crying in the wilderness: "Prepare The Way of The Lord, make straight in the desert a highway for our God."

41:1 "Keep silence before Me, O coastlands, and let the people renew their strength! Let them come near, then let them speak; let us come near together for judgment. 5 The coastlands saw it and feared, the ends of the earth were afraid; they drew near and came. 10 Fear not, For I am with you; be not dismayed, for I am your God. I will strengthen you, yes, I will help you, I will uphold you with 'My Righteous Right Hand.'"

11 "Behold, all those who were incensed against you shall be ashamed and disgraced; they shall be as nothing, and those who strive with you shall perish. 12 You shall seek them and not find them—those who contended with you. Those who war against you shall be as nothing, as a non-existent thing." 22 "Let them bring forth and show us what will happen; let them show the former things, what they were, that we may consider them, and know 'The Latter End of Them'; or declare to us things to come."

28 For I looked, and there was no man; I looked among them, but there was no counselor, who, when I asked of them, could answer a word. 42:22: But this is a people robbed and plundered; all of them are

snared in holes, and they are hidden in prison houses; they are for prey, and no one delivers; for plunder, and no one says, "Restore!"

Isaiah 43:5: Fear not, for I am with you, I will bring your descendants from the east, and gather them from the west; 6 I will say to the north, 'Give them up!' And to the south, 'Do not keep them back!' Bring My sons from afar, and My daughters from the ends of the earth—9 Let all the nations be gathered together, and let the people be assembled. Who among them can declare this, and show us former things? Let them bring out their witnesses, that they may be justified; or let them hear and say, "It Is Truth."

John 16:13: "However, when He, 'The Spirit of Truth,' has come, He will guide you into 'All Truth'; for He will not speak of His own authority, but whatever He hears He will speak; and He will tell you things to come. Romans 1:18: For The Wrath of God is revealed from heaven against all ungodliness and unrighteousness of men, who suppress 'The Truth' in unrighteousness. 20 For since 'The Creation of The World' His invisible attributes are clearly seen, being understood by the things that are made, even 'His Eternal Power and Godhead,' so that they are without excuse.

Romans 1:21: Because, although they knew God, they did not glorify Him as God, nor were they thankful, but became futile in their thoughts, and their foolish hearts were darkened. 22 Professing to be wise, they became fools. 28 And even as they did not like to retain God in their knowledge, God gave them over to a debased mind, to do the things which are not fitting, 29 Being filled with all unrighteousness, sexual immorality, wickedness, covetousness, maliciousness; full of envy, murder, strife, deceit, evil-mindedness; they are whisperers, 30 Backbiters, haters of God, violent, proud, boasters, inventors of evil, disobedient to parents, 31 Undiscerning, untrustworthy, unloving, unforgiving, unmerciful; 32 Who, knowing 'The Righteous Judgment of God,' that those who practice such things are deserving of death, not only do the same but also approve of those who practice them. 2:2 But we know that 'The Judgment of God' is according to 'The Truth' against those who practice such things.

Job 9:24: The earth is given into the hand of the wicked. He covers the faces of its judges. If it not He, who else could it be? Job 29:7: "When I went out to the gate by the city, when I took my seat in the open square. 8 The young men saw Me and hid, and the aged arose and stood. 9 The princes refrained from talking and put their hand on their mouth; 10 The voice of nobles was hushed, and their tongue stuck to the roof of their mouth.

11 When the ear heard then it blessed Me, and when the eye saw, then it approved Me; 12 Because I delivered the poor who cried out, the fatherless and the one who had no helper. 13 The blessing of a perishing man came upon Me, and I caused the widow's heart to sing for joy. 14 I put on righteousness, and it clothed Me; My Justice was like a robe and turban. 15 I was eyes to the blind, and I was feet to the lame. 16 I was 'A Father' to the poor, and I searched out the case that I did not know. 21 "Men listened to Me and wanted and kept silence for My Counsel. 22 After 'My Words' they did not speak again, and My speech settled on them as dew.

Psalms 89:6: For who in the heavens can be compared to The Lord? Who among the sons of the mighty can be likened to The Lord? 7 God is greatly to be feared in 'The Assembly of The Saints,' and to be held in reverence by all those around Him. 14 Righteousness and Justice are 'The Foundation of Your Throne'; Mercy and Truth go before Your face.

22 The enemy shall not outwit Him, nor the son of wickedness afflict Him. I will beat down His foes before His face, and plague those who hate Him. 24 "But My faithfulness and My mercy shall be with Him, and in My Name His horn shall be exalted. 25 Also I will set His hand over the sea, and 'His Right Hand' over the rivers.

Isaiah 16:5: In Mercy 'The Throne' will be established; and 'One' will sit on it 'In Truth,' in The Tabernacle of David, judging and seeking justice and hastening righteousness." 18:3: All inhabitants of the world and dwellers on the earth: when 'He Lifts Up A Banner' on the mountains, you see it; and when 'He Blows A Trumpet, you hear it. 7 In 'That Time' a present will be brought to The Lord of hosts from a people tall and smooth of skin, and from a people terrible from their beginning onward, a nation powerful and treading down, who land the rivers divide—to 'The Place of The Name of The Lord of hosts,' to Mount Zion.

Isaiah 19:11: "Surely the princes of Zoan are fools; Pharaoh's wise counselors give foolish counsel." How do you say to Pharaoh, 'I am the son of the wise, the son of ancient kings'? 18 In 'That Day' five cities in the land of Egypt will speak the language of Canaan and swear by The Lord of hosts; one will be called the city of destruction. 19 In 'That Day' there will be an altar to The Lord in the midst of the land of Egypt, and a pillar to The Lord at its border. 20 And it will be for a sign and for a witness to The Lord of hosts in the land of Egypt; for they will cry to The Lord because of the oppressors, and He will send them 'A Savior and A Mighty One,' and He will deliver them. 25 Whom The Lord of hosts shall bless, saying, "Blessed is Egypt My People, and Assyria the work of My hands, and Israel My Inheritance.

Isaiah 22:5: For it is a day of trouble and treading down and perplexity by The Lord of hosts in The Valley of Vision—breaking down the walls and of crying to the mountain. 9 You also saw the damage to The City of David, that it was great; and you gathered together the waters of the lower pool. 11 You also made a reservoir between the two walls for the water of the old pool, But you did not look to its Maker, nor did you have respect for Him who fashioned it long ago. 25 In 'That Day' says The Lord of hosts, 'the peg that fastened in the secure place will be removed and be cut down and fall, and the burden that was on it will be cut off; for The Lord of hosts has spoken.

24:1: Behold, The Lord makes the earth empty and make it waste, distorts its surface and scatters abroad its inhabitants. 3 The land shall be entirely emptied and utterly plundered, for The Lord has spoken 'This Word.' 5 The earth is also defiled under its inhabitants because they have transgressed 'The Laws,' changed the ordinance, broken The Everlasting Covenant. 6 Therefore the curse has devoured the earth, and those who dwell in it are desolate. Therefore, the inhabitants of the earth are burned, and few men are left. 10 The City of Confusion is broken down; every house is shut up, so that none may go in. 19 The earth is violently broken, the earth is split open, the earth is shaken exceedingly.

Isaiah 25:6: And in This Mountain The Lord of hosts will make for all people a feast of choice pieces, a feast of wines on the lees, of fat things full of marrow, of well-refined wines on the lees. 7 And He will destroy on this mountain the surface of the covering cast over all people, and the veil that is spread over all nations. 8 He will swallow up death forever, and The Lord God will wipe away tears from all faces; The rebuke of His people He will take away from all the earth; for The Lord has spoken.

9 And it will be said in 'That Day': "Behold, this is our God; we have waited for Him, and He will save us. This is The Lord; we have waited for Him; we will be glad and rejoice in 'His Salvation.'"

26:2: Open the gates, that 'The Righteous Nation' which keeps 'The Truth' may enter in. 3 You will keep Him in perfect peace, whose mind is stayed on You, because he trusts in You. 4 Trust in The Lord forever, for in YAH, The Lord, is everlasting strength. 7 The Way of The Just is 'Uprightness'; O Most Upright, you weigh 'The Path of The Just.'

I Corinthians 15:33: Do not be deceived; "evil company corrupts good habits." 34 Awake to righteousness, and do not sin, for some do not have The Knowledge of God. I speak this to your shame. 51 Behold, I tell you a mystery: We shall not all sleep, but we shall all be changed— 57 But thanks be to God, who gives us the victory through our Lord Jesus Christ. 58 Therefore My beloved brethren, be steadfast, immovable, always abounding in The Work of The Lord, knowing that your labor is not in vain in The Lord. 16:10: And if Timothy comes, see that he may be with you without fear; for he does The Work of The Lord, as I do also. 11 Therefore let no one despise him. But send him on his journey in peace, that he may come to me; for I am waiting for him with 'The Brethren.'

I Timothy 1:18: This charge I commit to you, son Timothy, according to the prophecies previously made concerning, that by them you may wage 'The Good Warfare.' 4:13: Till I come, give attention to reading, to exhortation, to doctrine. 6:10: For the love of money is a root of all kinds of evil, for which some have strayed from the faith in their greediness and pierced themselves with many sorrows. 20 O Timothy! Guard what was committed to your trust, avoiding the profane and idle babble and contradictions of what is falsely called knowledge—

Isaiah 64:4: For since the beginning of the world men have not heard nor perceived by the ear, nor has the eye seen any God besides You, who acts for the one who waits for Him. 5 You meet him who rejoices and does righteousness, who remembers You in Your Ways. You are indeed angry, for we have sinned—in these ways we continue; and we need to be saved. 7 And there is no one who calls on Your Name, who stirs himself up to take hold of You; for you have hidden Your face from us and have consumed us because of our iniquities. 9 Do not be furious, O Lord, nor remember iniquity forever; indeed, please look—we all are Your People!

65:1: "I was sought by those who did not ask of Me; I was found by those who did not seek Me, I said, "Here I Am, here I Am," to a nation that was not called by My Name. 2 I have stretched out My hands all day long to a rebellious people, who walk in a way that is not good, according to their own thoughts, 3 A people who provoke Me to anger continually to My Face; who sacrifice in gardens' and burn incense on alters of brick;" 6 "Behold, it is written before Me; I will not keep silence, but will repay—even repay into their bosom—7 Your iniquities and the iniquities of your fathers together," says The Lord, "Who have burn incense on the mountains and blasphemed Me on the hills; therefore I will measure their former work into their bosom.

8 Thus says The Lord: "As the new wine is found in the cluster, and one says, 'Do not destroy it, for a blessing is in it,' so will I do for My servants' sake, that I may not destroy them all. 9 I will bring forth descendants from Jacob, and from Judah an heir of My mountains; My Elect shall inherit it, and My servants shall dwell there. 10 Sharon shall be a fold of flocks, and the Valley of Achor a place for herds to lie down, for My People who have sought Me.

11 "But you are those who forsake The Lord, who forgot My Holy Mountain, who prepare a table for Gad, and who furnish a drink offering for Meni." 13 Therefore thus says The Lord God: Behold, My servants shall eat, but you shall be hungry; behold, My servants shall drink, but you shall be thirsty; behold, My servants shall rejoice, but you shall be ashamed; 14 Behold, My servants shall sing for joy of heart, but you shall cry for sorrow of heart, and wail for grief of spirit. 15 You shall leave your name as a curse to My chosen; for The Lord God will slay you and call His servants by another name; 16 So that he who blesses himself in the earth shall bless himself in 'The God of Truth'; because the former troubles are forgotten, and because they are hidden from My eyes.

Jeremiah 44:21: "The Incense that you burned in the cities of Judah and in the streets of Jerusalem, you and your fathers, your kings and your princes, and the people of the land, did not The Lord remember them, and did it not come into His mind? 22 So The Lord could no longer bear it, because the evil of your doings and because of the abominations which you have committed. Therefore, your land is a desolation, an astonishment. a curse, and without an inhabitant, as it is this day. Jeremiah

46:15: Why are your valiant men swept away? They did not stand because The Lord drove them away. 16 He made many fall; yes, one fell upon another, And they said, 'Arise! let us go back to our own people and to the land of our nativity from 'The Oppressing Sword."

Ezekiel 26:13: I will put an end to the sound of your songs, and the sound of you harps shall be heard no more. 18 Now the coastlands tremble on the day of your fall; the coastlands by the sea are troubled at your departure. 19 "For thus says The Lord God: 'When I make you a desolate city, like cities that are not inhabited, when I bring the deep upon you, and great waters cover you. 20 Then I will bring you down with those who descend into 'The Pit,' to the people of old, and I will make you dwell in the lowest part of the earth, in places desolate from antiquity, with those who go down to 'The Pit,' so that you may never be inhabited; and I shall establish Glory in The Land of The Living."

Psalms 102:16: For The Lord shall build up Zion; He shall appear in 'His Glory.' 17 He shall regard the prayer of the destitute and shall not despise their prayer. 18 This will be written for the generation to come, that a people 'Yet' to be created may Praise The Lord.

103:11: For as the heavens are high above the earth, so great is His Mercy toward those who fear Him; 12 As far as the east is from the west, so far has He removed our transgressions from us. 14 For He knows our frame, He remembers that we are dust. 17 But The Mercy of The Lord is from everlasting to everlasting on those who fear Him, and His righteousness to children's children. 18 To such as keep His covenant, and to those who remember His commandments to do them.

104:5: You who laid the foundations of the earth, so that it should not be moved forever, 6 You covered it with the deep as with garment; the waters stood above the mountains. 7 At your rebuke they fled; at 'The Voice' of Your thunder they hastened away. 8 They went up over the mountains; to the place which You founded for them. 14 He causes the grass to grow for the cattle, and vegetation for 'The Service of Man,' that he may bring forth food from the earth, 15 And wine that make glad the heart of man, oil to make his face shine, and bread which strengthens man's heart.

24 O Lord, how manifold are Your Works! In wisdom You have made them all. The earth is full of Your possessions—29 You hide Your face, They are troubled; You take away their 'Breath,' they die and

return to their dust. 30 You send forth 'Your Spirit,' they are created; and You renew the face of the earth. Revelation 21:1: Now I saw a new heaven and a new earth, for the first heaven and the first earth had passed away. Also, there was no more sea. 3 And I heard a loud voice from heaven saying, "Behold, 'The Tabernacle of God' is with men, and He will dwell with them, and they shall be His People. God Himself will be with them and be 'Their God.' 4 "And God will wipe away every tear from their eyes; there shall be no more death, nor sorrow, nor crying. There shall be no more pain, for the former things have passed away."

Proverbs 15:1: A soft answer turns away wrath, but a harsh word stirs up anger. 2 The tongue of the wise uses knowledge 'Rightly,' but the mouth of the fool pours forth foolishness. 3 The eyes of The Lord are in every place, keeping watch on the evil and the good. 5 A fool despises his father's instruction, but he who receives correction is prudent. 10 Harsh discipline is for him who forsakes the way, and he who hates correction will die. 11 Hell and destruction are before The Lord; so how much more the hearts of the sons of men.

14 The heart of him who has understanding seeks knowledge, but the mouth of fools feed on foolishness. 21 Folly is joy to him who is destitute of discernment, but a man of understanding walks uprightly. 23 A man has joy by the answer of his mouth, and 'A Word' spoken in due season, how good it is! 28 The heart of the righteous studies how to answer, but the mouth of the wicked pours forth evil.

33 The Fear of The Lord is 'The Instruction of Wisdom,' and before honor is humility. Proverbs 16:1: The preparations of the heart belong to man, but the answer of the tongue is from The Lord. 4 The Lord has made all for Himself, yes, even the wicked for 'The Day of Doom.' 6 In Mercy and Truth atonement is provided for iniquity; and by 'The Fear of The Lord' one departs from evil. 17 The Highway of The Upright is to depart from evil; he who keeps his way preserves his soul. 20 He who heeds 'The Word' wisely will find good, and whoever trusts in The Lord, happy is he.

Proverbs 16:27: An ungodly man digs up evil, and it is on his lips like a burning fire. 28 A perverse man sows' strife, and a whisperer separates the best of friends. 29 A violent man entices his neighbor and leads him in a way that is not good. 30 He winks his eye to devise perverse things; he pursues his lips and brings about evil. 17:18: He who begets a scoffer does so to his sorrow, and the father of a fool has no joy. 23 A wicked man accepts a bribe behind the back to pervert 'The Way of Justice.' 18:3: When the wicked comes, contempt comes also; and with dishonor comes reproach.

5 It is not good to show partiality to the wicked, or to overthrow the righteous in judgment. 17 The first one to plead 'His Cause' seems right, until his neighbor comes and examines him. 19:20: Listen to counsel and receive instruction, that you may be wise in your Latter Days. 21 There are many plans in a man's heart, nevertheless The Lord's Counsel—that will stand.

Psalms 37:14: The wicked have drawn the sword and bent their bow; to cast down the poor and needy, to slay those who are of 'Upright' conduct. 27 Depart from evil and do good, and dwell forevermore. 28 For The Lord loves justice and does not forsake His saints; they are preserved forever, but the descendants of the wicked shall be cut off. 35 I have seen the wicked in great power and spreading himself like a native green tree. 38 But the transgressors shall be destroyed together, the future of the wicked shall be cut off. 38:20: Those also who render evil for good, they are My adversaries, because I follow what is good.

Psalms 39:1: I said, "I will guard My ways, lest I sin with My tongue; I will restrain My mouth with a muzzle, while the wicked are before Me." 2 I was mute with silence, I help My peace even from good; and My sorrow was stirred up. 3 My heart was hot within Me; while I was musing, the fire burned, then I spoke with My tongue. 9 I was mute, I did not open my mouth, because it was You who did it. 10 Remove Your plague from Me; I am consumed by the blow of Your hand. 11 When with rebukes You correct man for iniquity, You make his beauty melt away like a moth; surely every man is vapor. Selah.

Psalms 40:6: Sacrifice and offering You did not desire; My ears You have opened, burnt offering and sin offering You did not require. 7 Then I said, "Behold I come; in the scroll of the book it is written of Me. 8 I delight to do Your Will, O My God, and Your Law is within My heart." 44:1: We have heard with our ears, O God, our fathers have told us, the deeds You did in their days, in days of old: 2 You drove out nations with Your Hand, but them You planted; You afflicted the peoples and cast them out. 3 For they did not gain possession of the land by their own sword, nor did their own arm save them; but it was 'Your Right Hand,' Your Arm, and The Light of Your Countenance, because You favored them.

Psalms 45:3: Gird 'Your Sword upon Your thigh, O Mighty One, with Your glory and Your majesty. 4 And in Your majesty ride prosperously because of Truth, Humility, and Righteousness; and Your Right Hand shall teach You awesome things. 5 Your arrows are sharp in the heart of their kings' enemies; the peoples fall under You. 6 Your Throne, O God, is forever and ever; 'A Scepter of Righteousness' is The Scepter of Your Kingdom. 7 You love righteousness and hate wickedness; therefore God, your God, has anointed You with 'The Oil of Gladness' more than Your companions.

Psalms 47:1: Oh, clap your hands, all you peoples! Shout to God with 'The Voice of Triumph'! 2 For The Lord Most High is awesome; He is A Great King over all the earth. 48:11: Let Mount Zion rejoice, let The Daughters of Judah be glad, because of Your Judgments. 51:6: Behold, You desire 'Truth' in the inward parts, and in the hidden part You will make Me to know 'Wisdom.' 10 Create in Me 'A Clean Heart,' O God, and Renew 'A Steadfast Spirit' within Me. 11 Do not cast Me away from Your presence, and do not take 'Your Holy Spirit' from Me. 17 The sacrifices of God are a broken spirit, a broken and a contrite heart—these, O God, You will not despise.

Isaiah 42:23: Who among you will give ear to "This'? Who will listen and hear for the time to come? 44:10: Who would form a god or mold an image that profit him nothing? 45:5: I am The Lord, and there is no other; there is no God besides Me. I will gird you, though you have not known Me. 7 I form the light and create darkness, I make peace and create calamity; I, The Lord, do all these things.

8 "Rain down, you heavens, from above, and let the skies pour down righteousness; let the earth open, let them bring forth Salvation, and let righteousness spring up together. I, The Lord, have created it. 12 I have made the earth and created man on it. I—My Hands—stretched out the heavens, and all their host I have commanded. 13 I have raised Him up in righteousness, and I will direct all His Ways; He shall build My city and let My exiles go free, not for price nor reward," says The Lord of hosts.

Isaiah 45:14: Thus says The Lord: "The labor of Egypt and merchandise of Cush and of the Sabeans, men of stature, shall come over to You, and they shall be Yours; they shall walk behind You, they shall come over in chains; and they shall bow down to You. They will make supplication to You, saying, 'Surely God Is In You,' and there is no other; there is no other God, who hide Yourself, O God of Israel, 'The Savior'!

19 I have not spoken in secret, in a dark place of the earth; I did not say to the seed of Jacob, 'Seek Me in vain'; I, The Lord, speak righteousness, I declare things that are right. 22 Look to Me, and be saved, all the ends of the earth! For I Am God, and there is no other. 23 I have sworn by Myself; 'The Word' has gone out of My mouth in righteousness, and shall not return, that to Me every knee shall bow, every tongue shall take an oath.

Isaiah 46:8: "Remember This, and show yourselves men; recall to mind, O you transgressors. 9 Remember the former things of old, for I Am God and there is no other; I Am God, and there is none like Me, 10 Declaring 'The End' from 'The Beginning,' and from ancient times things that are not yet done, saying, "My Counsel shall stand, and I will do all My pleasure." 11 Calling a bird of prey from the east, the man who executes My Counsel, from a far country. Indeed, I have spoken it; I will also bring it to pass, I have purposed it; I will also do it."

12 "Listen to Me, you stubborn hearted, who are far from righteousness: 13 I will bring My righteousness near, it shall not be far off; My Salvation shall not linger. And I will place Salvation in Zion, for Israel My Glory." Isaiah 48:6: "You have heard; see all 'This,' and will you not declare it? I have made you hear new things for 'This Time,' even hidden things, and you did not know them. 8 Surely you did not hear, surely you did not know; surely from long ago your ear was not opened. For I knew that you would deal treacherously and were called a transgressor from the womb. 10 Behold, I have refined you, but not as silver; I have tested you in the furnace of affliction.

11 For My Own Sake, for My own sake, I will do it; for how should My Name be profaned? And I will not give My Glory to another. 18 Oh, that you had heeded My Commandments! Then your peace would have been like a river, and your righteousness like the waves of the sea. Isaiah 49:6: Indeed He says, "It is a small thing that You should be My

Servant to raise up The Tribes of Jacob, and to 'Restore' the preserved ones of Israel; I will also give You as 'A Light' to the Gentiles, that You should be 'My Salvation' to The Ends of The Earth."

Jeremiah 51:44: I will punish Bel in Babylon, and I will bring out of his mouth what he has swallowed, and the nations shall not stream to him anymore, yes, the wall of Babylon shall fall. 45 "My people, go out of the midst of her! And let everyone deliver himself from 'The Fierce Anger of The Lord.' 49 As Babylon has caused the slain of Israel to fall, so at Babylon the slain of the earth shall fall. 50 You who have escaped 'The Sword,' get away! Do not stand still! Remember The Lord afar off, and let Jerusalem come to your mind.

51 We are ashamed because we have heard reproach, Shame has covered our faces, for strangers have come in The Sanctuaries of The Lord's House. Psalms 33:13: The Lord looks from heaven; He sees all the sons of men. 14 From the place of His dwelling He looks on all the inhabitants of the earth; 15 He fashions their heart individually; He considers all their works. 16 No king is saved by the multitude of an army; a mighty man is not delivered by great strength. 18 Behold, the eye of The Lord is on those who Fear Him, on those who hope in His mercy. 19 To deliver their soul from death, and to keep them alive in famine.

Psalms 34:7: The Angel of The Lord encamps all around those who Fear Him and delivers them. 11 Come, you children, listen to Me; I will teach you The Fear of The Lord. Proverbs 2:5: Then you will understand The Fear of The Lord and find The Knowledge of God. 6 For The Lord gives wisdom; from His mouth come knowledge and understanding; 7 He stores up 'Sound Wisdom' for the Upright; He is a shield to those who walk Uprightly; 21 For the Upright will dwell in the land, and the blameless will remain in it. Proverbs 3:11: My son, do not despise The Chastening of The Lord, nor detest His correction; 12 For who The Lord loves He corrects, just as a father the son in whom he delights.

Mark 16:6: But He said to them, "Do not be alarmed, you seek Jesus of Nazareth, who was crucified. "He is Risen!" He is not here. See the place where they laid Him. 14 Later He appeared to the eleven as they set at the table; and He rebuked their unbelief and hardness of heart, because they did not believe those who had seen Him after He had risen. Luke 24:37: But they were terrified and frightened, and supposed they had seen a spirit. 38 And He said to them, "Why are you troubled? And why do doubts arise in your hearts?" 39 "Behold My hands and My feet, that it is I Myself. Handle Me and see, for a spirit does not have flesh and bones as you see I have."

44 Then He said to them, "These are 'The Words' which I spoke to you while I was still with you, that all things must be fulfilled which were written in The Law of Moses and the prophets and the Psalms concerning Me." 45 And He opened their understanding, that they might comprehend 'The Scriptures.'

Revelation 11:4: These are the two olive trees and the two lampstands standing before The God of the earth. 5 And if anyone wants to harm them, fire proceeds from their mouth and devours their enemies, And if anyone wants to harm them, he must be killed in this manner. 6 These have power to shut heaven, so that no rain falls in the days of their prophesy; and they have power over waters to turn them to blood, and to strike the earth with all plagues, as often as they desire. Zechariah 4:14: So He said, "These are the two 'Anointed Ones,' who stand beside The Lord of The Whole Earth.

Zechariah 8:9: "Thus says The Lord of hosts: 'Let your hands be strong, you who have been hearing in 'These Days These Words' by the mouth of the prophets, who spoke in the day the foundation was laid for The House of The Lord of hosts, that the temple might be built.

Malachi 2:4: Then you shall know that I have sent this commandment to you, that 'My Covenant' with Levi may continue, says The Lord of hosts. 5 "My Covenant was with him, One of Life and Peace, and I gave them to him that he might 'Fear Me'; so he feared Me and was reverent before My Name. 6 The Law of Truth was in his mouth, and injustice was not found on His lips. He walk with Me in Peace and Equity and turned many away from iniquity.

Revelation 1:7: Behold, He is Coming with clouds, and every eye will see Him, even they who pierced Him. And all the tribes of the earth will mourn because of Him. Even so, Amen. 14 His head and hair were white like wool, as white as snow, and His eyes like a flame of fire; 15 His feet like fine brass, as if refined in a furnace, and 'His Voice' as the sound of many waters; 18 "I Am He who Lives, and was dead, and behold, I Am Alive Forevermore. Amen, And I have the keys of Hades and of death.

22:3: And there shall be no more curse, but The Throne of God and of The Lamb shall be in it. and His servants shall serve Him. 4 They shall see His face, and His name shall be on their foreheads, 16 "I, Jesus, have sent My angel to testify to you these things in the churches. I Am the Root and the offspring of David, the Bright and Morning star." Genesis 3:22: Then The Lord said, "Behold, the man has become like one of us, to know good and evil. And now, lest he put out his hand and take also of 'The Tree of Life,' and eat, and live forever." Genesis 4:7: "If you do well, will you not be accepted? And if you do not do well, sin lies at the door. And its desire is for you, but you should rule over it."

Philippians 1:6: Being confident of this very thing, that He who has begun a good work in you will complete it until "The Day of Jesus Christ'; 9 And this I pray, that your love may abound still more and more in knowledge and all discernment. 10 That you may approve the things that are excellent, that you may be sincere and without offense till 'The Day of Christ.' Isaiah 10:20: And it shall come to pass in 'That Day' the remnant of Israel, and such as escaped of The House of Jacob, will never again depend on him who defeated them, but will depend on The Lord, The Holy One of Isarel in Truth. 21 The remnant will return to the remnant of Jacob, to The Mighty God.

27 It shall come to pass in 'That Day' that his burden will be taken away from your shoulder, and his yoke from your neck, and the yoke will be destroyed because of 'The Anointing Oil.' 33 Behold, The Lord, The Lord of hosts, will lop off the bough with terror; those of high statue will be hewn down, and the haughty will be humbled. Ezekiel 23:25: I will set My jealousy against you, and they shall deal furiously with you; they shall remove your nose and your ears, and your remnant shall fall by 'The Sword'; they shall take your sons and your daughters, and your remnant shall be devoured by fire.

Ezekiel 23:32: "Thus says The Lord God: 'You shall drink of your sisters' cup, the deep and wide one; you shall be laughed to scorn and held in derision; it contains much. 33 You will be filled with drunkenness and sorrow, the cup of horror and desolation, the cup of your sister Samaria.'" 35 "Therefore thus says The Lord God: 'Because you have forgotten Me and cast Me behind your back, therefore you shall bear the penalty of your lewdness and your harlotry.'" 37 "For they committed adultery, and blood is on their hands. They have committed adultery with their idols, and even sacrificed their sons whom they bore to Me, passing them through the fire, to devour them."

38 "Moreover they have done this to Me: they have defiled My sanctuary on the same day and profaned My Sabbaths." 39 "For after they have slain their children for their idols, on the same day they came into My Sanctuary to profane it; and indeed thus they have done it in the midst of My House." 40 "Furthermore you sent men to come from afar, to whom a messenger was sent; and there they came. And you washed yourself for them, painted your eyes, and adorned yourself with ornaments." 41 "You sat on a stately couch, with a table prepared before it, on which you had set My incense and My oil." 45 "But righteous men will judge them after the manner of adulteresses, and after the manner of women who shed blood, because they are adulteresses, and blood is on their hands. 23:47: The assembly shall stone them with stones and execute them with their swords; they shall slay their sons and their daughters, and burn their houses with fire." 48 "Thus I will cause lewdness to cease from the land, that all women may be taught not to practice your lewdness." 49 They shall repay you for your lewdness, and you shall pay for your idolatrous sins, then you shall know that I Am The Lord God.

Isaiah 24:13: In your filthiness is lewdness. Because I have cleansed you, and you were not cleansed, you will not be cleansed of your filthiness anymore, till I have caused My Fury to rest upon you. 25:6: For thus says The Lord God: "Because you clapped your hands, stamped your feet, and rejoiced in heart with all your disdain for The Land of Israel. 7 "Indeed, therefore I will stretch out My hand against you, and give you as plunder to the nations; I will cut you off from the peoples, and I will cause you to perish from the countries; I will destroy you, and you shall know that I Am The Lord."

Leviticus 19:11: 'You shall not steal, nor deal falsely, nor lie to one another.' 15 'You shall do no injustice in judgment. You shall not be partial to the poor, nor honor the person of the mighty. In righteousness you shall judge your neighbor.' 18 'You shall not take vengeance nor bear any grudge against the children of your people, but you shall love your neighbor as yourself: I Am The Lord.'

31 'Give no regard to mediums and familiar spirits; do not seek after them; I Am The Lord your God.' 20:6: 'And the person who turns to mediums and familiar spirits, to prostitute himself with them, I will set My face against that person and cut him off from his people.' I Timothy 4:1: Now 'The Spirit' expressly says that in Latter Times some will depart from the faith, giving heed to deceiving spirits and doctrines of demons. 2 Speaking lies of hypocrisy, having their own conscience seared with a hot iron. II Peter 2:15: They have forsaken 'The Right Way' and gone astray, following the way of Balaam the son of Beor, who loved the wages of unrighteousness.

II Peter 3:1: Beloved, I now write to you this second epistle (in both of which I stir up 'Your Pure Mind' by way of reminder), 2 That you may be mindful of 'The Words' which were spoken before by the holy prophets, and of the commandment of us, the apostles of The Lord and Savior, 3 Know this first: that scoffers will come in 'The Last Days,' walking according to their own lusts, 4 And saying, "Where is 'The Promise' of His coming? For since the fathers fell asleep, all things continue as they were from the beginning of creation." 5 For this they willfully forget: that by The Word of God the heavens were of old, and the earth standing out of the water and in the water. 6 By which the world that then existed perished, being flooded with water.

7 But the heavens and the earth which now exist are kept in store by The Same Word, reserved for fire until The Day of Judgment and perdition of ungodly men. 11 Therefore, since all things will be dissolved, being on fire, and the elements will melt with fervent heat. 13 Nevertheless we, according to His Promise, look for new heavens and a new earth in which righteousness dwells. 17 You therefore, beloved, since you know this beforehand, beware lest you also fall from your own steadfastness, being led away with the error of the wicked.

I John 2:4: He who says, "I know Him," and does not keep His commandments, is a liar, and The Truth is not in him. 6 He who says he abides in Him ought himself also walk just as He walked. 9 He who says he is in 'The Light,' and hates his brother, is in darkness, until Now. 11 But he who hates his brother is in darkness and walks in darkness, and does not know where he is going, because the darkness has blinded his eyes.

15 Do not love the world or the things in the world, if anyone loves the world, the love of The Father is not in him. 16 For all that is in the

world—the lust of the flesh, the lust of the eyes, and the pride of life—is not of The Father but is of the world. 17 And the world is passing away, and the lust of it; but he who does The Will of God abides forever. 25 And this is 'The Promise' that He has promised us—Eternal Life.

Isaiah 60:1: Arise, shine, for your light has come! And The Glory of The Lord is risen upon you. 2 For behold, the darkness shall cover the earth, and deep darkness the people; but The Lord will arise over you, and His glory will be seen upon you. 3 The Gentiles shall come to your light, and kings to The Brightness of Your Rising. 15 "Whereas you have been forsaken and hated, so that no one went through you, I will make you Eternal Excellence, A joy of many generations."

18 Violence shall no longer be heard in your land, neither wasting nor destruction within your borders; but you shall call your walls Salvation, and your gates Praise. 21 Also your people shall all be righteous; they shall inherit the land forever, The Branch of My Planting, The Works of My Hands, that I may be glorified.

Isaish 61:1: "The Spirit of The Lord is upon Me, because The Lord has anointed Me to preach 'Good Tidings' to the poor; He has 'Sent Me' to heal the brokenhearted, to proclaim liberty to the captives, and the opening of the prison to those who are bound; 2 To Proclaim, The Acceptable Year of The Lord, and 'The Day of Vengeance' of our God; to comfort all who mourn. 3 To console those who mourn in Zion, to give them beauty for ashes, The Oil of Joy for mourning, The Garment of Praise for the spirit of heaviness; that they may be called 'Trees of Righteousness,' The Planting of The Lord, that He may be glorified. 4 And they shall rebuild the old ruins, they shall raise up the former desolations, and they shall repair the ruined cities, the desolations of many generations."

8 "For I, The Lord, love justice; I hate robbery for burnt offering, I will direct their work 'In Truth,' and will make with them 'An Everlasting Covenant.' 9 Their descendants shall be known among the Gentiles, and their offspring among the people, All who see them shall acknowledge them, that they are the posterity whom The Lord has blessed.

Isaiah 62:2: The Gentiles shall see Your righteousness, and all kings Your glory. You shall be called by a new name, which The Mouth of The Lord will name. 4 You shall no longer be termed forsaken, nor shall your land anymore be termed desolate; but you shall be called

Hephzibah, and your land Beulah; for The Lord delights in you, and your land shall be married. 5 For as a young man marries a virgin, so shall your sons marry you; and as The Bridegroom rejoices over The Bride, so shall your God rejoice over you.

Isaiah 62:6: I have set watchmen on your walls, O Jerusalem; They shall never hold their peace day or night. You who make mention of The Lord, do not keep silent. 7 And give Him no rest till He establishes and till He make Jerusalem a praise in the earth. 11 Indeed The Lord has proclaimed to the end of the world: "Say to The Daughters of Zion, surely your salvation is coming; behold, His reward is with Him, and His work before Him.'" 12 And they shall call them "The Holy People, The Redeemed of The Lord;" and you shall be called sought out, a city not forsaken.

Isaiah 11:1: There shall come forth 'A Rod' from the stem of Jesse, and 'A Branch' shall grow out of His roots. 2 The Spirit of The Lord shall rest upon Him, The Spirit of Wisdom and Understanding, The Spirit of Counsel and Might, The Spirit of Knowledge and of The Fear of The Lord. 12 He will set up 'A Banner' for the nations, and will assemble the outcasts of Israel, and gather together the dispersed of Judah from The Four Corners of the earth. 13:2: "Lift up 'A Banner' on the high mountain, raise your voice to them; wave your hand, that they may enter The Gates of The Noble.

Isaiah 13:13: Therefore I will shake the heavens, and the earth will move out of her place, in the wrath of The Lord of hosts and in the day of His Fierce Anger. 14:3: It shall come to pass in the day The Lord gives you rest from your sorrow, and from your fear and the hard bondage in which you were made to serve. 4 That you take up this proverb against the king of Babylon, and say: "How the oppressor has ceased, the golden city ceased! 5 The Lord has broken the staff of the wicked, the scepter of the rulers: 12 "How you are fallen from heaven, O Lucifer, son of the morning! How you are cut down to the ground, you who weakened the nations!"

24 The Lord of hosts has sworn, saying, "Surely, as I have thought, so it shall come to pass, and as I have purposed, so it shall stand: 16:5: In mercy The Throne will be established; and One will sit on it in 'Truth,' in The Tabernacle of David, judging and seeking justice and hastening righteousness."

Isaiah 16:7: Therefore Moab shall wail for Moab; everyone shall wail. For the foundations of Kir Harsath you shall mourn; surely, they are stricken. 8 For the fields of Heshbon languish, and the vine of Sibmah; the lords of the nations have broken down its choice plants, which has reached to Jazer and wandered through the wilderness. Her branches are stretched out, they are gone over the sea. 17:12: Woe to the multitude of many people who made noise like the roars of the seas, and to the rushing of nations that make a rushing like the rushing of mighty waters!

13 The nations will rush like the rushing of many waters; but God will rebuke them, and they will flee far away and be chased like the chaff of the mountains before the wind, like a rolling thing before the whirlwind. 14 Then behold, at eventide, trouble! And before the morning, he is no more. This is the portion of those who plunder us, and the lot of those who rob us.

Romans 11:15: For if their being cast away is 'The Reconciling of The World,' what will their acceptance be but life from the dead? 21 For if God did not spare the natural branches, He may not spare you either. 22 Therefore consider the goodness and severity of God; on those who fell, severity; but toward you, goodness, otherwise you also will be cut off. 25 For I do not desire, brethren, that you should be ignorant of 'This Mystery,' lest you should be wise in your own opinion, that blindness in part has happened to Israel until the fullness of the Gentiles has come in. 26 And so all Israel will be saved, as it is written: "The Deliverer will come out of Zion, and He will turn away ungodliness from Jacob, 27 For this is My Covenant with them, when I take away their sins."

33 Oh, the depth of the riches both of the wisdom and knowledge of God! How unsearchable are His judgments and His ways past finding out! 34 "For who has known the mind of The Lord? Or who has become His counselor?" 12:1: I beseech you therefore, brethren, that you present your bodies as living sacrifice, holy acceptable to God, which is your reasonable service. 2 And do not be conformed to this world, but be transformed by the renewing of your mind, that you may prove what is that good and acceptable and perfect will of God. Isaiah 66:22: "For as the new heaven and the earth which I will make shall remain before Me," says The Lord, So shall your descendants and your

name remain. 23 And it shall come to pass that from one new moon to another, and from one sabbath to another, all flesh shall come to worship before Me, says The Lord.

Daniel 2:20: Daniel answered and said: "Blessed be The Name of God forever and ever. for wisdom and might are His. 21 And He changes the times and the seasons; He removes kings and raises up kings; He gives wisdom to the wise and knowledge to those who have understanding, 22 He reveals deep and secret things; He knows what is in the darkness, and light dwells with Him.

Jeremiah 2:35: Yet you say, 'Because I am innocent, surely His anger shall turn from me.' Behold, I will plead My Case against you, because you say, 'I have not sinned.' 36 Why do you gad about much to change your way? Also, you shall be ashamed of Egypt as you were ashamed of Assyria. 37 Indeed you will go forth from him with your hands on your head; for The Lord has rejected your trusted allies, and you will not prosper by them.

3:14: "Return, O backsliding children," says The Lord; "for I am married to you. I will take you, one from a city and two from a family, and I will bring you to Zion. 15 "And I will give you shepherds according to My Heart, who will feed you with knowledge and understanding." 17 "At 'That Time' Jerusalem shall be called 'The Throne of The Lord,' and all nations shall be gathered to it, to The Name of The Lord, to Jerusalem. No more shall they follow the dictates of their evil heart.

Deuteronomy 32:29: Oh, that they were wise, that they understood 'This,' that they would consider their Latter End! 30 How could one chase a thousand, and two put ten thousand to flight, unless their Rock had sold them, and The Lord had surrendered them? 31 For their rock is not like our Rock, even our enemies themselves being judges. 32 For their vine is of the vine of Sodom and of the fields of Gomorrah; their grapes are grapes of gall; their clusters are bitter. 24 Their wine is the poison of serpents, and the cruel venom of cobras. 34 Is this not laid up in the store with me, sealed up among My treasures?

40 For I raise My hand to heaven, and say, as I Live Forever. Psalms 112:1: Praise The Lord! Blessed is the man who fears The Lord, who delights greatly in his commandments. 2 His descendants will be mighty on the earth; The Generation of The Upright will be blessed.

4 Unto the Upright there arises light in the darkness, He is gracious, and full of compassion, and righteous. 115:11: You who fear The Lord, trust in the Lord, He is their help and their shield. 12 The Lord has been mindful of us; He will bless us; He will bless The House of Israel; He will bless The House of Aaron. 13 He will bless those who fear The Lord, both small and great.

Psalms 116:8: For You have delivered my soul from death, my eyes from tears, and my feet from falling. 9 I will walk before The Lord in The Land of The Living. 12 What shall I render to The Lord for all His benefits toward me? 13 I will take up The Cup of Salvation and call upon The Name of The Lord. 18 I will pay my vows to The Lord now in the presence of all His People, 19 In the courts of The Lord's House, in the midst of You, O Jerusalem, Praise The Lord! Psalms 117:1: Praise The Lord, all you Gentiles! Laud Him, all you peoples! 2 For His merciful kindness is great toward us, and The Truth of The Lord endures forever. Praise The Lord!

118:6: The Lord is on my side; I will not fear. What can man do to me? 7 The Lord is for me among those who help me, therefore I shall see my desire on those who hate me. Job 27:12: Surely all of you have seen it; why then do you behave with complete nonsense? Job 30:2: Indeed, what profit is the strength of their hands to me? Their vigor has perished. 3 They are gaunt from want and famine, fleeing late to the wilderness, desolate and waste. 8 They were sons of fools, yes, sons of vile men; they were scourged from the land.

Job 34:22: There is no darkness nor shadow of death where the workers of iniquity may hide themselves. 25 Therefore He knows their works; He overthrows them in the night, and they are crushed, 26 He strikes them as wicked men in the open sight of others. 27 Because they turned back from Him, and would not consider any of His ways, 28 So that they caused the cry of the poor to come to Him; for He hears the cry of the afflicted.

29 When He gives quietness, who then can make trouble? And when He hides His face, who then can see Him, whether it is against a nation, or a man alone?—30 That the hypocrite should not reign, lest the people be ensnared. 33 Should He repay it according to your terms, just because you disavow it? You must 'choose,' and not I; therefore, speak what you know. 35:8: Your wickedness affects a man such as you,

and your righteousness a Son of Man. 9 "Because of the multitude of oppressions they cry out; they cry out for help because of the arm of the mighty.

Job 36:6: He does not preserve the life of the wicked but give justice to the oppressed. 12 But if they do not obey, they shall perish by 'The Sword,' and they shall die without knowledge. 16 "Indeed He would have brought you out of dire distress, into a broad place where there is no restraint; and what is set on your table would be full of richness. 19 Will your riches, or all the mighty forces, keep you from distress?

21 Take heed do not turn to iniquity, for you have 'chosen' this rather than affliction. Job 37:1: "At This also my heart trembles, and leaps from its place." Ecclesiastes 7:18: It is good that you grasp This, and also not remove your hand from the other; for he who 'Fears God' will escape them all. 20 For there is not a just man on earth who does good and does not sin.

Ecclesiastes 8:3: "Do not be hasty to go from His presence. Do not take your stand for an evil thing, for He does whatever pleases Him." 8 No one has power over 'The Spirit' to retain 'The Spirit,' and no one has power in the day of death. There is no release from that war, and wickedness will not deliver those who are given to it.

Ecclesiastes 12:3: In the day when the keepers of the house tremble, and the strong men bow down; when the grinders cease because they are few, and those that look through the windows grow dim; 4 When the doors are shut in the streets, and the sound of grinding is low; when one rises up at the sound of a bird, and all The Daughters of Music are brought low. 5 Also they are afraid of height, and of terrors in the way; when the almond tree blossoms, the grasshopper is a burden, and desire fails. For man goes to his eternal home, and the mourners go about the streets.

Isaiah 51:1: "Listen to Me, you who follow after righteousness, you who 'Seek The Lord': Look to the Rock from which you are hewn, and to the hole of 'The Pit' from which you were dug." 2 Look to Abraham your father, and to Sarah who bore you, for I called him alone, and blessed him and increased him. 3 For The Lord will comfort Zion, He will comfort all her waste places; He will make her wilderness like Eden, and her desert like The Garden of The Lord; joy and gladness will be found in it, thanksgiving and the voice of melody; 4 "Listen to Me, My people; and give ear to Me, O My Nation: for Law will proceed from Me, and I will make My Justice rest as a light of the peoples."

7 Listen to Me, you who know righteousness, you people in whose heart is My Law: do not fear the reproach of men, nor be afraid of their insults. 8 For the moth will eat them up as a garment, and the worm will eat them like wool; but My righteousness will be forever, and My Salvation from generation to generation to generation. 11 So 'The ransomed of The Lord shall return, and 'Come' to Zion with singing, with everlasting joy on their heads. They shall obtain joy and gladness; sorrow and sighing shall flee away.

Psalms 102:16: For The Lord shall build up Zion; He shall appear in His Glory. 19 For He looked down from the height of His Sanctuary; from heaven The Lord viewed the earth. 20 To hear the groaning of the prisoner, to release those appointed to death, 21 To declare The Name of The Lord in Zion, and His praise in Jerusalem 22 When the peoples are gathered together, and the kingdoms, to serve The Lord.

II Chronicles 13:8: "And now you think to withstand The Kingdom of The Lord, which is in the hand of the sons of David; and you are a great multitude, and with you are the gold calves which Jeroboam made for us as gods." 10 "But as for us, The Lord is our God, and we have not forsaken Him; and the priests who minister to The Lord are the sons of Aaron, and the Levites attend to their duties." 12 "Now look, God Himself is with as our head, and His priest with sounding trumpets to sound 'The Alarm' against You, O Children of Israel, do not fight against The Lord of your fathers, for you shall not prosper!"

II Chronicles 14:2: Asa did what was good and right in The Eyes of The Lord his God. 3 For he removed the altars of the foreign gods and the high places and broke down the sacred pillars and cut down the wooden images. 4 He commanded Judah 'To Seek The Lord God' of their fathers, and 'To Observe The Law and The Commandments.' 5 He also removed the high places and the incense altars from all the cities of Judah, and the kingdom was quiet under him. 6 And he built fortified cities in Judah, for the land had rest; he had no war in those years, because The Lord had given him rest.

II Chronicles 16:12: And in the thirty-ninth year of his reign, Asa became diseased in his feet, and his malady was severe, yet in his disease He did not seek The Lord, but the physicians. 13 So Asa rested with his fathers; he died in the forty-first year of his reign. 17:1: Then Jehoshaphat his son reigned in his place and strengthened himself against Israel. 3 Now, The Lord was with Jehoshaphat, because he walked in the former ways of his father David; he did not seek Baals, 4 But sought The God of his father, and walked in His commandments and not according to the acts of Israel.

II Chronicles 19:4: So Jehoshaphat dwelt at Jerusalem; and he went out again among the people from Beersheba to the mountains of Ephraim and brought them back to The Lord God of their fathers. 5 Then he set judges in the land throughout all the fortified cities of Judah, city by city. 6 And he said to the judges, "Take heed to what you are doing, for you do not judge for man but for The Lord, who is with you in the judgment. 7 "Now therefore, let 'The Fear of The Lord' be upon you; take care and do it, for there is no iniquity with The Lord our God, no partiality, nor taking of bribes."

9 And he commanded them, saying, "Thus you shall act in 'The Fear of The Lord, faithfully and with a Loyal Heart'; 10 "Whatever case comes to you from your brethren who dwells in their cities, whether of bloodshed or offenses against the law or commandment, against statutes or ordinances, you shall warn them, lest they trespass against The Lord and wrath comes upon you and your brethren. Do This, and you will not be guilty.

Isaiah 25:10: For on This Mountain 'The Hand of The Lord Will Rest,' and Moab shall be trampled down, under Him, as straw is trampled down for the refuse heap. 11 And He will spread out His Hands in their midst as a swimmer reaches out to swim, and He will bring down their pride together with the trickery of their hands. 26:5: "For He brings down those who dwell on high, the lofty city; He lays it low; He lays it low to the ground, He brings it down to the dust. 6 The foot shall tread it down—the feet of the poor and the steps of the needy."

11 Lord, when Your Hand is lifted up, they will not see. But they will see and be ashamed for their envy of people; yes, the fire of Your enemies shall devour them. 16 Lord, in trouble they have visited You, they poured out a prayer when Your chastening was upon them.

Jeremiah 22:10: Weep not for the dead, nor bemoan him; weep bitterly for him who goes away, for he shall not return no more, nor see his native country. 17 "Yet your eyes and your heart are for nothing but your covetousness, for shedding innocent blood, and practicing oppression and violence." 21 I spoke to you in your prosperity, but you said, 'I will not hear.' This has been your manner from your youth, that you did not 'Obey My Voice.'

22 The wind shall eat up all your rulers, and your lovers shall go into captivity; surely then you will be ashamed and humiliated for all your wickedness. 23:10: For the land is full of adulterers; for because of 'A Curse' the land mourns. The pleasant places of the wilderness are dried up. Their course of life is evil, and their might is not right. 17 They continually say to those who despise Me, 'The Lord has said, "You shall have peace"'; and to everyone who walks according to the dictates of his own heart, 'No evil shall come upon you.'"

20 The Anger of The Lord will not turn back until He has executed and performed the thoughts of His heart. In 'The Latter Days' you will understand it perfectly. 23 "Am I a God near at hand," says The Lord, "And not a God afar off? 24 Can anyone hide himself in secret places, so I shall not see him?" says The Lord. 27 "Who try to make My People forget My Name by their dreams which everyone tells his neighbor, as their fathers forgot My Name for Baal." 35 "Thus every one of you shall say to his neighbor, and everyone to his brother, 'What has The Lord answered?' and, 'What has The Lord spoken?'"

Jeremiah 24:6: 'For I will set My eyes on them for good, and I will bring them back to this land; I will build them and not pull them down, and I will plant them and not pluck them up.' 7 'Then I will give them a heart to know Me, that I am The Lord; and they shall be My People, and I will be their God, for they shall return to Me with their whole heart.' Jeremiah 33:6: 'Behold, I will bring it health and healing; I will heal them and reveal to them the abundance of peace and Truth. 8 I will cleanse them from all their iniquity by which they have sinned against Me, and I will pardon all their iniquities by which they have sinned and by which they have transgressed against Me.'

9 "Then it shall be to Me 'A Name of Joy, A Praise, and An Honor' before all the nations of the earth, who shall hear all the good that I do to them; they shall fear and tremble for all the goodness and all the prosperity that I provide for it! 10 "Thus says The Lord: 'Again there shall be heard in this place—of which you say, "It is desolate, without

man and without beast"—in the Cities of Judah, in the streets of Jerusalem that are desolate, without man and without inhabitant and without beast, 11 'The Voice of Joy' and 'The Voice of Gladness,' 'The Voice of The Bridegroom' and 'The Voice of The Bride,' the voice of those who will say: "Praise The Lord of hosts, for The Lord is good, for His mercy endures forever"—and of these who will bring the sacrifice of praise into The House of The Lord. For I will cause the captives of the land to return as at the first! says The Lord."

14 'Behold, the days are coming,' says The Lord, 'that I will perform that good thing which I have promised to The House of Israel and to The House of Jacob:' 15 'In those days and at that time I will cause to grow up to David 'A Branch of Righteousness'; He shall execute judgment and righteousness in the earth. 17 "For thus says The Lord: David shall never lack a man to sit on 'The Throne of The House of Israel.'

Psalms 112:1: Praise The Lord! Blessed is the man who Fears The Lord, who delights greatly in His Commandments. 2 His descendants will be mighty on earth; the generation of The Upright will be blessed. 4 Unto The Upright, there rises light in darkness; He is gracious and full of compassion, and righteous. 8 Surely, He will never be shaken; the righteous will be in everlasting remembrance. 7 He will not be afraid of evil tidings; His heart is steadfast, trusting in The Lord.

8 His heart is established; He will not be afraid, until He sees His desire upon His enemies. 9 He has dispersed abroad; He has given to the poor; His righteousness endures forever; His horn will be exalted with honor. 10 The wicked will see it and be grieved; he will gnash his teeth and melt away; the desire of the wicked shall perish.

Proverbs 12:6: The words of the wicked are, "Lie and wait for blood," but the mouth of The Upright will deliver them. 7 The wicked are overthrown and are no more, but the house of the righteous will stand. 13 The wicked is ensnared by the transgression of his lips, but the righteous will come through trouble. 17 He who speaks Truth declares righteousness, but a false witness, deceit. 20 Deceit is in the heart of those who devise evil, but Counselors of Peace have joy. 22 Lying lips are an abomination to The Lord, but these who deal truthfully are His delight. 26 The righteous should 'choose' his friend carefully, for the way of the wicked leads them astray. 28 In The Way of Righteousness is life, and in its pathway, there is 'no death.'

Proverbs 13:1: A wise son heeds his father's instruction, but a scoffer does not listen to rebuke. 12 Hope deferred makes the heart sick, but when the desire comes, it is 'A Tree of Life.' 13 He who despises 'The Word' will be destroyed, but he who fears the commandment will be rewarded. 14 The Law of The Wise is a fountain of life, to turn one away from the snares of death. 14:16: A wise man fears and departs from evil, but a fool rage and is self-confident. 15:5: A fool despises his father's instruction, but he who receives correction is prudent. 10 Harsh discipline is for him who forsakes 'The Way,' and he who hates correction will die.

Proverbs 16:2: All the ways of a man are pure in his own eyes, but The Lord weighs 'The Spirit.' 4 The Lord has made all things for Himself, yes, even the wicked for The Day of Doom. 6 In mercy and Truth atonement is provided for iniquity; and by The Fear of The Lord one departs from evil. 17:4: An evildoer give heed to false lips; a liar listens eagerly to a spiteful tongue. 15 He who justifies the wicked, and he who condemns the just, both of them alike are an abomination to The Lord.

Isaiah 34:1: Come near, your nations, to hear; and heed, you people! Let the earth hear, and all that is in, the world and all things that come forth from it. 2 For The Indignation of The Lord is against all nations, and His Fury against all their armies; He has utterly destroyed them, He has given them over to 'the slaughter.' 3 Also their slain shall be thrown out; their stench shall rise from their corpses, and the mountains shall be melted with their blood. 4 All the host of heaven shall be dissolved, and the heavens shall be rolled up like a scroll; all their host shall fall down as the leaf from the vine, and as fruit falling from a fig tree. 5 "For 'My Sword' shall be bathed in heaven; indeed, it shall come down on Edom, and on the people of 'My Curse,' for Judgment. 8 For it is the day of The Lord's vengeance, the year of recompense for The Cause of Zion. 12 They shall call its nobles to the kingdom, but none shall be there, and all its princes shall be nothing.

II Corinthians 11:2: For I am jealous for you with 'Godly jealousy.' For I have betrothed you to 'One' husband, that I may present you as a chaste virgin to Christ. 3 But I fear, lest somehow, as the serpent deceived Eve by his craftiness, so your mind may be corrupted from the simplicity that is in Christ. 6 Even though I am untrained in speech, yet I am not in knowledge. But we have been thoroughly manifested among you in all things. 7 Did I commit sin in humbling myself that you might be exalted, because I preached The Gospel of God to you free of charge?

13 For such are false apostles, deceitful workers, transforming themselves into apostles of Christ. 14 And no wonder! For Satan himself transforms himself into an angel of light. 15 Therefore it is no great thing if his ministers also transform themselves into ministers of righteousness, whose end will be according to their works.

I Thessalonians 2:3: For our exhortation did not come from error or uncleanness, nor was it in deceit. 4 But as we have been approved by God to be entrusted with The Gospel, even so we speak, not as pleasing men, but God who tests our hearts. 5 For neither at any time did we use flattering words, as you know, nor a cloak for covetousness—God Is Witness. 19 For what is our hope, or joy, or crown of rejoicing? Is it not even you in the presence of our Lord Jesus Christ at His Coming?

3:1: Therefore, when we could no longer endure it, we thought it good to be left in Athens alone, 2 And sent Timothy, our brother and minister of God, and our fellow laborer in The Gospel of Christ, to establish you and encourage you concerning your faith. 3 That no one should be shaken by these afflictions; for you yourselves know that we are appointed to 'This.'

II Timothy 1:12: For This reason I also suffer these things; nevertheless, I am not ashamed, for I know whom I have believed and am persuaded that He is able to keep what I have committed to Him until 'That Day.' Philemon 1:8: Therefore, though I might be very bold in Christ to command you what is fitting, 9 Yet for 'Love's Sake' I rather appeal to you—being such a one as Paul, the aged, and now also a prisoner of Jesus Christ. Colossians 1:8: Who also declared to us your love in 'The Spirit.' 9 For this reason we also, since the day we heard it, do not cease to pray for you, and ask that you might be filled with The Knowledge of His Will in all wisdom and spiritual understanding.

12 Giving thanks to The Father who has qualified us to be partakers of the inheritance of the saints in the light. 13 He has delivered us from the power of darkness and conveyed us into The Kingdom of The Son of His love. 25 Of which I became a minister to the stewardship from God which was given to me for you, to fulfill 'The Word of God.' 26

'The Mystery' which has been hidden from ages and from generations, but now has been revealed to His saints.

Nahum 1:2: God is jealous, and The Lord avenges, The Lord avenges and is furious. The Lord will take vengeance on His adversaries, and He reserves Wrath for His enemies. 3 The Lord is slow to anger and great in power, and will not at all acquit the wicked, The Lord has His way in the whirlwind and in the storm, and the clouds are the dust of His feet.

11 From you comes forth one who plots evil against The Lord, a wicked counselor. 12 Thus says The Lord: "Though they are safe, and likewise many, yet in this manner they will be cut down when he passes through. Though I have afflicted you, I will affect you no more, 13 For now I will break off his yoke from you and burst your bonds apart." 14 The Lord has given a command concerning you: "Your name shall be perpetuated no longer. Out of the house of your gods I will cut off the craved image and the molded image. I will dig your grave, for you are vile." 15 Behold, on the mountains the feet of Him who brings good tidings, who proclaims peace! O Judah, keep your appointed feasts, perform your vows. For the wicked one shall no more pass through you; he is utterly cut off.

Mark 7:3: For the Pharisees and all the Jews do not eat unless they wash their hands in a special way, holding the tradition of the elders. 4 When they come from the marketplace, they do not eat unless they wash. And there are many other things which they have received and hold, like the washing of cups, copper vessels, and couches. 6 He answered and said to them, "Well did Isaiah prophesy of you hypocrites, as it is written: 'This people honors Me with their lips, but their heart is far from Me.' 7 "And in vain they worship Me, teaching as doctrines 'the commandments of men,'" 8 "For laying aside 'The Commandment of God,' you hold the tradition of men—the washing of pitchers and cups, and many other such things you do."

9 He said to them, "All too well you reject 'The Commandment of God,' that you may keep your tradition." 13 "Making 'The Word of God' of no effect through your tradition which have been handed down. And many such things you do." 20 And He Said, "What comes out of a man, that defiles a man." 21 "For from within, out of the heart of men, proceed evil thoughts, adulteries, fornications, murders, 22

Thieves, covetousness, wickedness, deceit, lewdness, an evil eye, blasphemy, pride, foolishness." 23 "All these evil things come from within and defile a man."

James 1:13: Let no one say when he is tempted, "I am tempted by God," for God cannot be tempted by evil, nor does He Himself tempt anyone. 14 But each one is tempted when he is drawn away by his own desires and enticed. 15 Then, when desire has conceived, it gives birth to sin, and sin, when it is full-grown, brings forth death. 21 Therefore lay aside all filthiness and overflow of wickedness, and receive with meekness 'The Implanted Word,' which is able to save your souls.

2:19: You believe that there is 'One God,' you do well; even the demons believe—and tremble! 3:14: But if you have bitter envy and self-seeking in your hearts, do not boast and lie against 'The Truth.' 15 This wisdom does not descend from above, but is earthly, sensual, demonic. 16 For where envy and self-seeking exist, confusion and every evil thing are there. 3:17: But 'The Wisdom' that is from above is first Pure, then Peaceable, gentle, willing to yield, full of mercy and good fruits, without partiality and without hypocrisy. 4:7: Therefore submit to God, Resist the devil and he will flee from you. 8 Draw near to God and He will draw near to you. Cleanse your hands, you sinners; and purify your hearts, you double-minded.

5:1: Come now, you rich, weep and howl for your miseries that are coming upon you! 2 Your riches are corrupted, and your garments are moth-eaten. 3 Your gold and silver are corroded, and their corrosion will be a witness against you and will eat your flesh like fire. You have heaped up treasure in 'The Last Days.' 4 Indeed the wages of the laborers who moved your fields, which you kept back by fraud, cry out; and the cries of the reapers have reached the ears of The Lord of Sabaoth. 5 You have lived on the earth in pleasure and luxury; you have fattened your hearts as in 'A Day of Slaughter.' 6 You have condemned; you have murdered The Just; he does not resist you.

Matthew 4:16: The people who sat in darkness have seen 'A Great Light,' and upon those who say in the region and Shadow of Death light has dawned. 5:17: "Do not think that I came to destroy The Law of the prophets, I did not come to destroy but to fulfill." 18 "For assuredly, I say to you, till heaven and earth pass away, one jot or one tittle will by no means pass from The Law till all is fulfilled." 19

"Whosoever therefore breaks one of the least of these commandments, and teaches men so, shall be called least in The Kingdom of Heaven, but whoever does and teaches them, he shall be called Great in The Kingdom of heaven." 20 "For I say to you, that unless your righteousness exceeds the righteousness of the scribes and Pharisees, you will by no means enter The Kingdom of heaven."

Matthew 7:21: Not everyone who says to Me, 'Lord, Lord,' shall enter The Kingdom of Heaven, but he who does The Will of My Father in heaven. 22 "Many will say to Me in that day, 'Lord, Lord,' have we not prophesied in Your Name, cast out demons in Your Name, and done many wonders in Your Name?" 23 "And then I will declare to them, 'I never knew you; depart from Me, you who practice lawlessness!'"

Psalms 7:9: Oh, let the wickedness of the wicked come to an end, but establish The Just; for The Righteous God tests the hearts and minds. 10 My defense is of God, who Saves 'The Upright' in heart. 11 God is 'A Just Judge,' and God is angry with the wicked every day. 12 If he does not turn back, He will sharpen 'His Sword'; He bends His bow and makes it ready.

Ezekiel 30:3: For 'The Day' is near, even The Day of The Lord is near, it will be a day of clouds, the time of the Gentiles. 4 'The Sword' shall come upon Egypt, and great anguish shall be in Ethiopia, when the slain fall in Egypt, and they take away her wealth, and her foundations are broken down. 5 Ethiopia, Libya, Lydia, and all the mingled people, Chub, and the men of the lands who are allied, shall fall with them by 'The Sword.' 6 Thus says The Lord: "Those who uphold Egypt shall fall, and the pride of her power shall come do. From Migdol to Syene those within her shall fall by 'The Sword," says The Lord God.

Zephaniah 1:4: "I will stretch out My Hand against Judah, and against all the inhabitants of Jerusalem. I will cut off 'Every Trace' of Baal from this place, the name of the idolatrous priests with the pagan priests—6 Those who have turned back from following The Lord, and have not sought The Lord, nor inquired of Him." 12 "And it shall come to pass at 'That Time' I will search Jerusalem with lamps, and punish the men who are settled in complacency, who say in their heart, 'The Lord will not do good, nor will He do evil,'

2:3: Seek The Lord, all you meek of the earth, who have upheld His Justice. Seek Righteousness, Seek Humility. It may be that you will be hidden in The Day of The Lord's Anger. 9 Therefore, as I live, says The Lord of hosts, The God of Israel, "Surely Moab shall be like Sodom, and the people of Ammon like Gomorrah—overrun with weeds and salt pits, and a perpetual desolation, The residue of My people shall plunder them, and the remnant of My people shall possess them." 10 This they shall have for their pride, because they have reproached and made arrogant threats against The People of The Lord of hosts. 11 The Lord will be awesome to them, for He will reduce to nothing all the gods of the earth; people shall worship Him, each one from his place, indeed all the shores of the nations, 3:5: The Lord is righteous in her midst, He will do no unrighteous. Every morning He brings His Justice to Light; He never fails, but the unjust knows no shame. 7 I said, 'Surely you will fear Me, and receive instruction—so that her dwelling would not be cut off, despite everything for which I punished her, but they rose early and corrupted all their deeds.

Zephaniah 3:8: "Therefore wait for Me," says The Lord, "Until the day I rise up for plunder; My determination is to gather the nations to 'My Assembly of Kingdoms,' to poor on them 'My Indignation,' all My Fierce Anger; all the earth shall be devoured with the fire of My jealousy." 9 "For then I will restore to The People A Pure Language, that they may call on 'The Name of The Lord,' to serve Him with one accord." 12 I will leave in your midst a meek and humble people, and they shall trust in The Name of The Lord." 13 "The remnant of Israel shall do no unrighteousness and speak no lies, nor shall a deceitful tongue be found in their mouth; for they shall feed their flocks and lie down, and no one shall make them afraid."

14 "Sing, O Daughter of Zion! Shout, O Israel! Be glad and rejoice with all your heart, O Daughter of Jerusalem! 17 The Lord your God in your midst, The Mighty One, will save; He will rejoice over you with gladness, He will quiet you with 'His Love,' He will rejoice over you with singing."

Proverbs 1:2: To know wisdom and instruction, to perceive 'The Words of Understanding,' 3 To receive 'The Instruction of Wisdom, Justice, Judgment, and Equity'; 4 To give prudence to the simple, to the young man knowledge and discretion—5 A wise man will hear and increase learning, and a man of understanding will attain wise counsel, 6 To understand a proverb and an enigma, the words of the wise and their riddles. 7 The Fear of The Lord is the beginning of knowledge, but fool despise wisdom and instruction.

20 Wisdom calls aloud outside; she raises her voice in the open squares. 21 She cries out in the chief concourses, at the openings of the gates in the city she speaks her words: 2:6: For The Lord gives wisdom; from His mouth comes knowledge and understanding; 7 He stores up 'Sound Wisdom' for The Upright; He is a shield to those who walk Uprightly; 8 He guards 'The Paths of Justice' and preserves 'The Way of His Saints.' 9 Then you will understand righteousness, and justice, equity and 'Every Good Path.' 20 So you may walk in The Way of Goodness and keep to The Paths of Righteousness. 21 For the Upright will dwell in the land, and the blameless will remain in it.

Jeremiah 11:6: Then The Lord said to Me, "Proclaim all 'These Words' in the cities of Judah and in the streets of Jerusalem, saying: 'Hear the words of 'This Covenant' and 'Do Them.' 7 'For I earnestly Exhorted your fathers in the day I brought them up out of the land of Egypt, until 'This Day,' rising early and Exhorting, saying, "Obey My Voice."' 11 Therefore thus says The Lord: "Behold, I will surely bring calamity on them which they will not be able to escape; and though they cry out to Me, I will not listen to them."

12 "Then the cities of Judah and the inhabitants of Jerusalem will go and cry out to the gods to whom they offer incense, but they will not save them at all in the time of their trouble." 13 "For according to the number of your cities were your gods, O Judah; and according to the number of the streets of Jerusalem you have set up altars to that shameful thing, altars to burn incense to Baal."

Deuteronomy 18:9: "When you come into the land which The Lord your God is giving you, you shall not learn to follow the abominations of those nations." 10 "There shall not be found among you anyone who makes his son or his daughter pass through the fire, or one who practices witchcraft, or a soothsayer, or one who interprets omens, or a sorcerer," 11 "Or one who conjures spells, or a medium, or a spiritism, or one who calls up the dead." 12 "For all who do these things are an abomination to The Lord, and because of these abominations The Lord your God drives them out from before you."

14 "For these nations which you will dispossess listened to soothsayers and diviners; But as for you, The Lord your God has not appointed such for you." 15 "The Lord your God will raise up for A Prophet, from your brethren like me from your midst, from your brethren, Him shall you Hear, 19 'And it shall be that whoever will not hear 'My Words,' which He speaks in My Name, I will require it of him.'

Ezekiel 11:15: "Son of man, your brethren, your relatives, your countrymen, and all The House of Israel in its entirely, all those about whom the inhabitants of Jerusalem have said, 'Get far away from The Lord; this land has been given to us as a possession!'" 12:2: "Son of man, you dwell in the midst of a rebellious house, which has eyes to see but does not see, and ears to hear but does not hear; for they are a rebellious House." 25 "For I am The Lord, I speak, and 'The Word' which I speak will come to pass; it will no more be postponed; for in your days, O rebellious House, I will say 'The Word' and 'Perform It,'" says The Lord God.

27 "Son of man, Look, The House of Israel is saying, 'The vision that He sees is for many days from now, and He prophesies of times far off.'" 28 "Therefore say to them, 'Thus says The Lord God: "None of My Words will be postponed any more, but The Word which I speak will be done,'" says The Lord God. 14:3: "Son of man, these men have set up their idols in their hearts and put before them that which causes them stumble into iniquity." Should I let Myself be inquired of all by them? 6 Therefore say to The House of Israel, Thus says The Lord God: "Repent, turn away from your idols, and turn your faces away from all your abominations." 13 "Son of man, when a land sins against Me by 'Persistent Unfaithfulness,' I will stretch out My Hand against it; I will cut off its supply of bread, send famine on it, and cut off man and beast from it."

Ezekiel 16:49: "Look, this was the iniquity of your sister Sodom: she and her daughter had pride, fullness of food, and abundance of idleness; neither did she strengthen the hand of the poor and needy." 50 "And they were haughty and committed abomination before Me; therefore I took them away as I saw fit." 56 "For your sister Sodom was not a byword in your mouth in the days of your pride," 18:19: "Yet you say, 'Why should the son not bear the guilt of the father'?" Because the son has done what is lawful and right, and has kept all My Statutes and observed them, he shall surely live.

Ecclesiastes 1:4: One generation passes away, and another generation comes, but the earth abides forever. 9 That which has been is what will be, that which is done is what will be done, and there is nothing new under the sun. 10 Is there anything of which it may be said, "See, this is new"?" It has already been in ancient times before us. 11 There is no remembrance of former things, nor will there be any remembrance of things that are to come by those who will come after.

13 And I set My heart to seek and search out by Wisdom concerning all that is done under heaven; this burdensome task God has given to The Sons of Man, by which they may be exercised. 2:3: I searched in My heart how to gratify My flesh with wine, while guiding My heart with Wisdom, and how to hold on folly, till I might see what was good for The Sons of Men to do under heaven all the days of their lives. 13 Then I saw that Wisdom excels folly as light excels darkness.

5:1: Walk prudently when you go to The House of God; and draw 'near to hear' rather than to give sacrifice of fools, for they do not know that they do evil. 2 Do not be rash with your mouth and let not your heart utter anything hastily before God. For God is in heaven, and you on earth; therefore, let your words be few. 3 For a dream comes through much activity, and a fool's voice is known by his many words.

Titus 1:10: For there are many insubordinates both idle talkers and deceivers, especially those of the circumcision, 11 Whose mouths must be stopped, who subvert whole households, teaching things which they ought not, for the sake of dishonest gain. 13 This Testimony is True. Therefore, rebuke them sharply, that they may be sound in the faith. 14 Not giving heed to Jewish fables and commandments of men who turn you from The Truth.

2:1: But as for you, speak the things which are proper for 'Sound Doctrine': 12 Teaching us that, denying ungodliness and worldly lusts, we should live soberly, righteously, and godly in the present age. 13 Looking for the blessed hope and glorious appearing of our Great God and Savior Jesus Christ. 14 Who gave Himself for us, that He might redeem us for every lawless deed and purify for Himself 'His Own Special People,' zealous for 'Good Works.'

Psalms 33:13: The Lord looks from heaven; He sees all the sons of men. 14 From the place of His dwelling He looks on all the inhabitants of the earth. 15 He fashions their hearts individually; He considers all their works. Psalms 90:3: You turn man to destruction, and say, "Return, O Children of Men." 4 For a thousand years in Your sight are like yesterday when it is past, and like a watch in the night.

7 For we have been consumed by Your anger, and by Your wrath we are terrified. 11 Who knows the power of Your anger? For as the fear of You, so is Your wrath. Psalms 92:9: For behold, your enemies, O Lord, for behold, Your enemies shall perish; all the workers of iniquity shall be scattered. 13 Those who are planted in The House of The Lord shall flourish in The Courts of Our God. 14 They shall still bear fruit in old age; they shall be fresh and flourishing. 15 To declare that The Lord is Upright; He is My Rock, and there in no unrighteousness in Him. Psalms 94:14: For The Lord will not cast off His people, nor will he forsake His Inheritance. 15 But judgment shall return to righteousness, and all The Upright in heart will follow it.

Deuteronomy 12:8: "You shall not at all do as we are doing here today—every man doing whatever is right in his own eyes—" 9 "For as yet you have not come to The Rest and The Inheritance which The Lord your God is giving you. 28 "Observe and Obey all 'These Words' which I command you, that it may go well with you and your children after you forever, when you do what is Good and Right in The Sight of The Lord your God."

Jeremiah 4:19: O My soul, My soul! I am pained in My very heart! My heart make a Noice in Me; I cannot hold My peace, because you have heard, O My soul, The Sound of The Trumpet, the alarm of war. 22 "For My people are foolish, they have not known Me, They are silly children, and they have no understanding. They are wise to do evil, but to do good they have no knowledge." 5:1: "Run to and from through the streets of Jerusalem; see now and know; and seek in her open places if you can find a man, if there is anyone who executes judgment, who Seeks The Truth, and I will pardon her." Isaiah 4:2: "Speak comfort to Jerusalem, and cry out to her, that her warfare is ended, that her iniquity is pardoned, she has received from The Lord's Hand double for all her sins."

Isaiah 40:3: The Voice of One crying in the wilderness: "Prepare The Way of The Lord; make straight in the desert a highway for our God." 5 The Glory of The Lord shall be revealed, and all flesh shall see it together; for The Mouth of The Lord has spoken. 12 Who has measured the waters in The Hallow of His Hand, measured heaven with a span and calculated the dust of the earth in a measure? Weighed the mountains in scales and the hills in a balance? 13 Who has directed The Spirit of The Lord, or as His counselor has taught Him?

22 It is He who sits above the circle of the earth, and its inhabitants are like grasshoppers, who stretches out the heavens like a curtain, and spreads them out like a tent to dwell in. 26 Lift up your eyes on high, and see who has created these things, who brings out their host by number; He calls them all by name, by The Greatness of His Might and The Strength of His Power; not one is missing.

28 Have you not known? Have you not heard? The Everlasting God, The Lord, The Creator of the ends of the earth, neither faints nor is weary. His Understanding is unsearchable. 29 He gives power to the weak, and to those who have no might He increases strength. 30 Even the youth shall faint and be weary, and the young men shall utterly fail. 31 But those who wait on The Lord shall renew their strength; they shall mount up with wings like eagles, they shall run and not be weary, they shall walk and not faint.

Jeremiah 51:10: The Lord has revealed our righteousness. Come and let us declare in Zion The Work of The Lord our God. 47 Therefore behold, The days are coming that I will bring judgment on the carved images of Babylon; her whole land shall be ashamed, and all her slain shall fall in her midst. 48 Then the heavens and the earth and all that is in them shall sing joyously over Babylon; for her plunderers shall come to her from the north. says The Lord. 49 As Babylon has caused the slain of Israel to fall, so at Babylon the slain of all the earth shall fall.

50 You who have escaped The Sword, get away! Do not stand still! Remember The Lord afar off, and let Jerusalem come to your mind. 55 Because The Lord is plundering Babylon and silencing her loud voice, though her waves roar like great waters, and the noise of their voice is uttered. 57 "And I will make drunk her princes and wisemen, her governors, her deputies, and her mighty men. And they shall sleep A Perpetual Sleep and not wake up," says The King, whose Name is The Lord of hosts.

Revelation 17:1: Then one of the seven angels who had seven bowls came and talked with me, "Come, I will show you the judgment of the great harlot who sets on many waters." 2 With whom the kings of the earth committed fornication, and the inhabitants of the earth were made drunk with the wine of her fornication." 4 The women was arrayed in purple and scarlet, and adorned with gold and precious stones and pearls, having in her hand a golden cup full of abominations and the filthiness of her fornication, 5 And on her forehead was written: 'Mystery' Babylon the great, the mother of harlots and the abomination of the earth.

6 I saw the woman, drunk with the blood of the saints and with the blood of the martyrs of Jesus. And when I saw her, I marveled with great amazement. 14 "These will make war with The Lamb, and The Lamb will overcome them, for He is The Lord of lords and King of Kings; and those who are with Him are Called, Chosen, and Faithful."

18:8: "Therefore her plagues will come in one day—death and mourning and famine. And she will be utterly burned with fire, for Strong is The Lord God who judges her." 23 "The light of the lamp shall not shine in you anymore, and 'The Voice of The Bridegroom and Bride' shall not be heard in you anymore. For your merchants were the great men of the earth, for by your sorcery all the nations were deceived. 19:2: "For True and Righteous are His Judgments, because He has judged the great harlot who corrupted the earth with her fornication; and He has avenged on her the blood of His servants shed by her."

Jeremiah 6:19: Hear, O earth! Behold, I will certainly bring calamity on this people—the fruit of their thoughts, because they have not heeded My Words nor My Law but rejected it. 7:12: "But go now to My place which was in Shiloh, where I set My Name at 'The First' and see what I did to it because of the wickedness of My people Israel." 9:5: "Your Dwelling place is in the midst of deceit; through deceit they refuse to know Me," says The Lord. 14 "But they have walked according to the dictates of their own hearts and after Baals, which their fathers taught them."

Jeremiah 2:5: Thus says The Lord: "What injustice have your fathers found in Me, that they have gone far from Me, have followed idols, and have become idolaters? 6 Neither did they say, 'Where is The Lord, who brought us up out of the land of Egypt, who led us through the wilderness, through a land of drought and The Shadow of Death, through a land that no one crossed and where no one dwelt?' 8 The priest did not say, 'Where is The Lord'? And those who handle 'The

Law' did not know Me; the rulers also transgressed against Me; the prophets prophesied by Baal and walked after things that do not profit. 17 Have you not brought This on yourself, in that you have forsaken The Lord your God when He led you in 'The Way'? 19 Your own wickedness will correct you, and your backslidings will rebuke you. Know therefore and see that it is an evil and bitter thing that you have forsaken The Lord your God, and The Fear of Me is not in you," says The Lord God of hosts.

Jeremiah 2:21: Yet I had planted you A Noble Vine, a seed of high quality. How then have you turned before Me into the degenerate plant of an alien vine? 23 "How can you say, 'I am not polluted, I have not gone after the Baals'? See your way in the valley; know what you have done: you are a swift dromedary breaking loose in her ways. 25 Withhold your foot from being unshod, and your throat from thirst. But you said, "There is no hope, No! For I have love aliens, and after them I will go."

26 "As the thief is ashamed when he is found out, so is The House of Israel ashamed; they and their kings and their princes, and their priests and their prophets. 27 Saying to a tree, 'You are my father,' and to a stone, 'You gave birth to me.' For they have turned their back to Me, and not their face. But in the time of their trouble they will say, 'Arise and save us.'

Acts 8:21: "You have neither part or portion in 'This Matter,' for your heart is not right in The Sight of God." 22 "Repent therefore of this your wickedness and pray God if perhaps the thought of your heart may be forgiven you." 23 "For I see that you are poisoned by bitterness and bound by iniquity."

Romans 14:10: But why do you judge your brother? Or why do you show contempt for your brother? For we shall all stand before The Judgment Seat of Christ. 11 For it is written: "As I live, says The Lord, every knee shall bow to Me, and every tongue shall confess to God." 12 So then each of us shall give account of himself to God. 13 Therefore let us not judge one another anymore, but rather resolve This, not to put a stumbling block or A Cause to fall in our brother's way.

15:4: For whatever things were written before were written for our learning, that we through the patience and comfort of The Scriptures might have 'Hope.' 5 Now may The God of Patience and Comfort grant you to be like-minded toward one another, according to Christ Jesus. 8 Now I say that Jesus Christ has become a servant to the circumcision for The Truth of God, To confirm The Promises made to the fathers, 9 And that the Gentiles might glorify God for His mercy, as it is written: "For this reason I will confess to You among the Gentiles and sing to Your Name.

Romans 15:12: And again, Isaiah says: "There shall be 'A Root of Jesse,' and He who shall 'Rise to Reign' over the Gentiles, in Him the Gentiles 'Shall Hope,'" 15 Nevertheless, brethren, I have written more boldly to you on some points, as reminding you, because of 'The Grace' given to Me by God. 20 And so I have made in 'My Aim' to preach The Gospel, not where Christ was named, lest I should build another man's foundation. 21 But as it is written: "To whom He was not announced, they shall see; and those who have not heard shall understand."

I Corinthians 1:22: For Jews request a sign, and Greeks seek after wisdom; 23 But we preach Christ crucified, to Jews 'a stumbling block' and to the Greeks 'foolishness,' 24 But to those who are 'Called,' both Jews and Greeks, 'Christ the Power of God and The Wisdom Of God.' 2:7 But we speak 'The Wisdom of God' in a mystery, 'The Hidden Wisdom' which God ordained before 'The Ages' for our glory, 8 Which none of the rulers of 'this age' knew, for had they known, they would have crucified 'The Lord of Glory.'

2:9: But as it is written: "Eye has not seen, nor ear heard, nor have entered into the heart of man the things which God has prepared for those who love Him." 10 But God has revealed them to us through 'His Spirit,' for 'The Spirit' searches all things, yes, The Deep Things of God. 4:14: I do not write these things to shame you, but as My Beloved Children 'I Warn You'! 15 For though you might have ten thousand instructors in Christ, yet you do not have many 'Fathers'; for in Christ Jesus I have 'Begotten You' through The Gospel.

Galatians 4:4: But when The Fulness of The Time had come, God sent forth His Son, born of a woman, but under The Law. 5 To redeem those who were under The Law, that we might receive 'The Adoption' as Sons. 9 But now after you have known God, or rather are 'Known By God,' How is it that you turn again to the weak and beggarly elements, to which you desire again to be in bondage?

10 You observe days and months and seasons and years. 11 I am afraid for you, lest I have labored for you in vain. 12 Brethren, I urge you to become like Me, for I became like you, you have not injured Me at all. 16 Have I therefore become your enemy because I tell you 'The Truth'? 20 I would like to be present with you now and to change My Tone; for I have doubts about you. 21 Tell Me, you who desire to be under The Law, do you not 'Hear The Law'?

22 For it is written that Abraham had two sons: the one by a bondwoman, the other by a freewoman. 23 But he who was of the bondwoman was born according to the flesh, and he of the freewomen through 'Promise.' 29 But, as he who was born according to the flesh then persecuted him who was born according to 'The Spirit,' 'Even So It Is Now.' 5:1 Stand fast therefore in 'The Liberty' by which Christ has made us free, and do not be entangled again with a yoke of bondage.

Galatians 5:4: You have become estranged from Christ, you who attempt to be justified by law; you have fallen from grace. 6:7: Do not be deceived, God is not mocked; for whatever a man sows, that he will also reap. 8 For he who sows to his flesh will of the flesh reap corruption, but he who sows to 'The Spirit' will of The Spirit' reap 'Everlasting Life.'

Hebrews 3:7: Therefore, as The Holy Spirit says: "Today if you will hear His Voice, 8 Do not harden your hearts as in the rebellion, in the day of trial in the wilderness, 9 Were your fathers tested Me, tried Me, and saw My Works forty years. 10 Therefore I was angry with that generation, and said, 'They always go astray in their heart, and they have not known My Ways': 11 So I swore in My Wrath, "They shall not enter My Rest."'

4:1: Therefore, since 'A Promise' remains of entering His Rest let us Fear lest any of you seem to have come short of it. 12 For The Word of God is living and powerful, and sharper than any two-edged sword, piercing even to the division of soul and spirit, and of joints and marrow, and is 'A Discerner' of the thoughts and intents of the heart.

Micah 3:6: "Therefore you shall have night without vision, and you shall have darkness without divination; the sun shall go down on the prophets, and the day shall be dark for them. 7 So the Seers shall be ashamed, and the diviners abashed; indeed, they shall all cover their lips; for there is no answer from God.

Isaiah 37:28: "But I know your dwelling place, you're going out and you're coming in, and your rage against Me. 29 Because your rage against Me and your tumult have come to My ears, therefore I will put My hook in your nose and My bridle in your lips, and I will turn you back by the way which you come."

40:26: Lift up your eyes on high, and see who has created these things, who brings out their host by number; He call them all by name, by The Greatness of His Might and The Strength of His Power; not one is missing. 41:5: The coastlands saw it and feared, the ends of the earth were afraid; they drew near and came. 43:2: When you pass through the waters, I will be with you; and through the rivers, they shall not overflow you. When you walk through the fire, you shall not be burned, nor shall the flame scorch you.

Isaiah 41:27: The first time I said to Zion, 'Look, there they are!' And I will give to Jerusalem 'One' who brings good tidings. 28 For I looked, and there was no man; I looked among them, but there was no counselor, who, when I asked of them, could answer a word. 29 Indeed they are all worthless; their works are nothing; their molded images are 'wind and confusion.'

Job 16:2: "I have heard many such things; miserable comforters are you all! 3 Shall 'words of wind' have an end? Or what provokes you that you should answer?" 6 "Though I speak, My grief is not relieved; and if I remain silent, how am I eased? Psalms 25:14: The secret of The Lord is with those who fear Him, and He will show them His Covenant. 19 Consider My enemies, for they are many; and they hate Me with cruel hatred. 27:13: I would have lost heart, unless I had believed that I would see The Goodness of The Lord in The Land of The Living.

Psalms 27:1: The Lord is My Light and My Salvation; whom shall, I fear? The Lord is The Strength of My Life; of whom shall I be afraid? 5 For in The Time of Trouble He shall hide me in His Pavilion; in The Secret Place of His Tabernacle, He shall hide me; He shall set me high upon a rock.

28:6: Blessed be The Lord, because He has heard 'The Voice of My Supplications'! 49:6: "Indeed He says, 'It is too small a thing that You should be My Servant to raise up the tribes of Jacob, and to 'Restore' the preserved ones of Israel; I will also give You as A Light to the Gentiles, that You should be My Salvation to the ends of the earth.

Isaiah 49:8: Thus says The Lord: "In an acceptable time I have heard You, and in The Day of Salvation I have helped You; I will preserve You and give You as A Covenant to the people, To Restore The Earth, to cause them to inherit the desolate heritages: 10 They shall neither hunger nor thirst, neither heat nor sun shall strike them, for He who has mercy on them will lead them, even by the springs of water He will guide them. 16 See, I have inscribed you on 'The Palms of My hand'; your walls are continually before Me. 50:6: I gave My back to those who struck Me, and My cheeks to those who plucked out My beard; I did not hide My face from shame and spitting.

Isaiah 51:4: "Listen to Me, My People, and give ear to Me, O My Nation; for Law will proceed from Me, and I will make My Justice rest as A Light of the peoples. 11 So The Ransomed of The Lord shall Return, and 'Come To Zion' with singing, with Everlasting Joy on their heads. They shall obtain joy and gladness; sorrow and sighing shall flee away. 16 And I have put My Words in your mouth; I have covered you with The Shadow of My Hand, that I may plant the heavens, lay the foundations of the earth, and say to Zion, 'You are My People.'

52:3: For thus says The Lord: "You have sold yourselves for nothing, and you shall be Redeemed Without Money." 54:13: All your children shall be taught by The Lord, and great shall be the peace of your children. 14 In righteousness you shall be established; you shall be far from oppression, for you shall not fear; and from terror, for it shall not come near you.

Isaiah 56:1: Thus says The Lord: "Keep Justice, and do righteousness, for My Salvation is about to come, and My righteousness to be revealed. 57:1: The righteous perish, and no man takes it to heart; merciful men are taken away, while no one considers that 'The Righteous is Taken Away' from evil.

Isaiah 59:19: So shall they fear The Name of The Lord from the west, and His Glory from the rising of the sun; when the enemy comes in like a flood, The Spirit of The Lord will lift up a standard against him. 21 "As for Me," says The Lord, "This is My Covenant with them: My Spirit who is upon you, and My Words which I have put in your mouth, shall not depart from your mouth, nor from the mouth of your descendants, nor from the mouth of your descendants' descendants," says The Lord. "From This Time and Forevermore."

65:6: "Behold, it is written before Me: I will not keep silence, but will repay—even repay into their bosom—7 Your iniquities and the iniquities of your fathers together," says The Lord, "who have burned incense on the mountains and blasphemed Me on the hills; therefore I will measure their former work into their bosom." 9 I will bring forth descendants from Jacob, and from Judah an heir on My Mountains; My Elect shall inherit it, and My Servants shall dwell there. 17 "For behold, I create New heavens and a New earth; and the former shall Not be remembered or come to mind."

Jeremiah 24:6: 'For I will set My eyes on them for good, and I will bring them back to 'This Land'; I will build them and not pull them down, and I will plant them and not pluck them up.' 7 Then I will give them a heart to know Me, that I Am The Lord; and they shall be My People, and I will be their God, for they shall Return to Me with their whole heart.

31:12: Therefore they shall Come and Sing in The Height of Zion, streaming to The Goodness of The Lord—for wheat and new wine and oil, for the young of the flock and the herd; their souls shall be like a well-watered garden, and they shall sorrow no more at all. 21 "Set up signposts, make landmarks; set your heart toward the highway, The Way in which you went. Turn back, O Virgin of Israel, turn back to these your cities. 23 Thus says The Lord of hosts, The God of Israel: "They shall again use 'This Speech' in the land of Judah and in its cities, when I bring back their captivity: 'The Lord bless you, O Home of Justice, and Mountain of Holiness!'"

Jeremiah 32:39: "Then I will give them 'One Heart and One Way,' that they may fear Me forever, for the good of them and their children after them." 40 'And I will make 'An Everlasting Covenant' with them, that I will not turn away from doing them good; but I will put My Fear in their hearts so that they will not depart from Me.'

Jeremiah 33:10: "Thus says The Lord: Again there shall be heard in 'This Place'—of which you say, It is desolate without man and without beast—in the cities of Judah, in the streets of Jerusalem that are desolate, without man and without inhabitant and without beast, 11 'The Voice of Joy and The Voice of Gladness, The Voice of The Bridegroom and The Voice of The Bride, The Voice of those who will say: Praise The Lord of hosts, for The Lord is good, for His mercy endures forever—and of those who will bring The Sacrifice of Praise into The House of The Lord. For I will cause the captives of the land to Return as at "The First,' says The Lord."

Ezekiel 7:23: 'Make a chain, for the land is filled with crimes of blood, and the city is full of violence. 24 Therefore I will bring the worst of the Gentiles, and they will possess their houses; I will cause the pomp of the strong to cease, and their holy places shall be defiled. 25 Destruction comes, they will seek peace, but there shall be none.

I Thessalonians 5:3: For when they say, "Peace and Safety!" Then sudden destruction comes upon them, as labor pains upon a pregnant woman. And they shall not escape. I Thessalonians 1:9: These shall be punished with everlasting destruction from The Presence of The Lord and from The Glory of His Power. 2:7: For the mystery of lawlessness is already at work; only he who now restrains will do so until he is taken out of the way. 8 And then the lawless one will be revealed, whom The Lord will consume with The Breath of His Mouth and destroy with The Brightness of His Coming.

Revelations 18:4: And I heard another Voice from heaven saying, "Come out of her, My People, lest you share in her sins, and lest you receive of her plagues." 5 "For her sins have reached to heaven, and God has remembered her iniquities." 23 "The light of a lamp shall not shine in you anymore, and The Voice of The Bridegroom and Bride shall not be heard in you anymore. For your merchants were the great men of the earth. For by your sorcery all the nations were deceived.

Proverbs 15:3: The eyes of The Lord are in every place, keeping watch on the evil and the good. 10 Harsh discipline is for him who forsakes 'The Way,' and he who hates correction will die. 16:1: The preparations of the heart belong to man, but the answer of the tongue is from The Lord. 4 The Lord has made all for Himself, yes, even the wicked for The Day of Doom.

Isaiah 59:13: In transgressing and lying against The Lord, and departing from our God, speaking oppression and revolt, conceiving and uttering from the heart words of falsehood. 14 Justice is turned back, and righteousness stands afar off; for Truth is fallen in the street, and equity cannot enter. 61:8: "For I, The Lord, love Justice; I hate robbery for burnt offering; I will direct their works in Truth and will make with them 'An Everlasting Covenant.'" 11 For as the earth brings forth its bud, as the garden causes the things that are sown in it to spring forth, so The Lord God will cause Righteousness and Praise to spring forth before all nations.

Ezekiel 36:23: "And I will sanctify My Great Name, which has been profaned among the nations, which you have profaned in their midst; and the nations shall know that I Am The Lord," says The Lord God. "When I Am hallowed in you before their eyes." 34 "The desolate land shall be tilled instead of lying desolate in the sight of all who pass by." 35 "So they will say, 'This land was desolate has become like The Garden of Eden; and the wasted, desolate and ruined cities are now fortified and inhabited,' 36 Then the nations which are left all around you shall know that I, The Lord, have rebuilt the ruined places and planted what was desolate. I, The Lord, have spoken it, and I will do it.

Ezekiel 38:19: "For in My jealousy and in The Fire of My Wrath I have spoken; 'Surely in 'That Day' there shall be a 'Great Earthquake' in The Land of Israel, 20 'So that the fish of the sea, the birds of heavens, the beast of the field, all creeping things that creep on the earth, and All Men who are on the face of the earth shall shake at My Presence. The mountains shall be thrown down, the steep places shall fall, and every wall shall fall to the ground.'" 23 "Thus I will Magnify Myself and Sanctify Myself, and I will be known in the eyes of many nations. Then they shall know that I Am The Lord.'"

39:8: "Surely it is coming, and it shall be done," says The Lord God. "This is 'The Day' of which I have spoken. 21 "I will set My Glory among the nations; all the nations shall see My Judgment which I have executed, and My Hand which I have laid on them." 23 "The Gentiles shall know that The House of Israel went into captivity for their iniquity; because they were unfaithful to Me, therefore I hid My Face from them, I gave them into the hand of their enemies, and they all fell by The Sword."

Isaiah 3:12: As for My People, children are their oppressors, and women rule over them. O My People! Those who lead you cause you to err and destroy 'The Way' of your paths. 13 The Lord stands up to plead and stands to Judge the people. 13:11: "I will punish the world for its evil, and the wicked for their iniquity; I will halt the arrogance of the proud and will lay low the haughtiness of the terrible."

Psalms 99:1: The Lord Reigns; let the people tremble! He dwells between the cherubim; let the earth be moved! 2 The Lord is great in

Zion, and He is high above all the peoples. 3 Let them praise Your great and awesome name—He is Holy. 4 The King's strength also love justice; You have established equity; You have executed justice and righteousness in Jacob. 5 Exalt The Lord our God, and worship at His footstool—He is Holy.

Psalms 11:1: In The Lord I put My trust; how can you say to My soul' "Flee as a bird to your mountain"? Nahum 1:15: Behold, on the mountains the feet of Him who brings good tidings, who proclaims Peace! O Judah, keep your appointed feast, perform your vows. For the wicked one shall no more pass through you; he is utterly cut off. Zephaniah 3:11: In 'That Day' you shall not be shamed for any of your deeds in which you transgress against Me, for then I will take away from your midst those who rejoice in your pride, and you shall no longer be haughty in 'My Holy Mountain.'

Jeremiah 5:7: "How shall I pardon you for this? Your children have forsaken Me and sworn by those that are not gods. When I had fed them to the full, then they committed adultery and assembled themselves by troops in the harlots' houses. 8 They were like well-fed lusty stallions: everyone neighed after his neighbor's wife. 14 Therefore thus says The Lord God of hosts: "Because you speak this word, behold, I will make My Words in your mouth fire, and this people wood, and it shall devour them."

I Samuel 12:7: "Now therefore, stand still, that I may reason with you before The Lord concerning all the righteous acts of The Lord which He did to you and your fathers." 14 "If you fear The Lord and serve him and obey His Voice, and do not rebel against The Commandment of The Lord, then both you and the king who reigns over you will continue following The Lord your God." 15 "However, if you do not obey The Voice of The Lord, but rebel against The Commandment of The Lord, then The Hand of The Lord will be against you, as it was against your fathers."

16 Now Therefore, stand and see This Great Thing which The Lord will do before your eyes; 23 Moreover, as for Me, far be it from Me that I should sin against The Lord in ceasing to pray for you; but I will teach you The Good and The Right Way; 24 Only Fear The Lord, and serve Him in Truth with all your hearts; for consider what great things He has done for you.

I Samuel 12:25: "But if you still do wickedly, you shall be swept away, both you and your king." 15:23: For rebellion is as the sin of witchcraft, and stubbornness is as iniquity and idolatry. Because you have rejected The Word of The Lord, He also has rejected you from being king. 24 Then Saul said to Samuel, "I have sinned, for I have transgressed The Commandment of The Lord, and your words, because I feared the people, and obey their voice." 25 "Now therefore, please pardon my sin, and return with me, that I may worship The Lord." 28 So Samuel said to him, "The Lord has torn The Kingdom of Israel from you today, and has given it to a neighbor of yours, who is better then you."

18:14: And David behaved wisely in all his ways, and The Lord was with him. Psalms 4:3: "But know that The Lord has set apart for Himself Him Who is Godly" 'The Lord Will Hear When I Call To Him.' 5:3: My Voice you shall hear in the morning, O Lord; in the morning I will direct it to You, and I will look up. 6:9: The Lord has heard my supplication; The Lord will receive my prayer.

Psalms 10:12: Arise, O Lord! Do not forget the humble. 17 Lord, You have heard the desire of the humble; You will prepare their heart; You will cause Your ear to hear. 12:1: Help, Lord, for The Godly Man ceases! For The Faithful disappear from among the sons of men. 17:1: Hear 'A Just Cause,' O Lord, attend to my cry; give ear to my prayer which is not from deceit lips. 2 Let 'My Vindication' come from Your Presence; let Your Eyes look on the things that are Upright. 8 Keep Me as The Apple of Your Eye; hide me under The Shadow of Your Wings. 15 As for Me, I will see Your Face in righteousness; I shall be satisfied when I awake in Your Likeness.

Psalms 20:6: "Now I know that The Lord 'Saves His Anointed'" He will answer him from His Holy Heaven with 'The Saving Strength of His Right Hand.' 21:3: For You meet him with The Blessings of Goodness; you set a crown of pure gold upon his heart. 4 He ask life from You, and You gave to him—length of days forever and ever.

Isaiah 53:3: He is despised and rejected by men, a man of sorrows and acquainted with grief, And we hid, as it were, our faces from Him; He was deposed, and we did not esteem Him. 5 But He was wounded for our transgressions, He was bruised for our iniquities; the chastisement for our peace was upon Him, and by His stripes we are healed. 7 He was oppressed, and He was afflicted, yet He open not His mouth; He was led as 'A Lamb' to the slaughter, and as a sheep before its shearers is silent, so He opened not His mouth.

Matthew 26:3: Then the chief priests and the scribes, and the elders of the people assembled at the palace of the high priest, who was called Caiaphas. 4 And plotted to take Jesus by trickery and kill Him. 59 Now, the chief priests, the elders, and all the council sought false testimony against Jesus to put Him to death. John 18:11: So Jesus Said to Peter, "Put you sword into its sheath. Shall I not drink 'The Cup' which My Father has given Me?" 13 And they led Him away to Annas first, for he was the father-in-law of Caiaphas who was high priest that year. 14 Now it was Caiaphas who advised the Jews that it was expedient that 'One Man' should die for the people. 23 Jesus answered him, "If I have spoken evil, bear witness of the evil; but if well, why do you strike Me?"

24 Then Annas sent Him bound to Caiaphas the high priest. 28 Then they led Jesus from Caiaphas to the Praetorium, and it was early morning. But they themselves did not go into the Praetorium, lest they should be defiled, but they might eat The Passover. 37 Pilate therefore said to Him, "Are You a king then?" Jesus answered, "You say rightly that I Am a King. For 'This Cause' I was born, and for 'This Cause' I have come into the world, that I should bear witness to "The Truth." Everyone who is of "The Truth" hears 'My Voice.' John 19:19: Now Pilate wrote a title and put it on 'The Cross.' And the writing was: JESUS OF NAZARETH, THE KING OF THE JEWS.

20:20: When He said 'This,' He showed them His Hands and His Side. Then the disciples were glad when they saw The Lord. 20:30: And Truly Jesus did many other signs in the presence of His disciples, which are not written in 'This Book'; 31 But these are written that you may believe that Jesus is The Christ, The Son of God, and that believing you may have 'Life' in His Name. 21:25: And there are also many other things that Jesus did, which if they were written one by one, I suppose that even the world itself could not contain the books that would be written. Amen.

Psalms 76:1: In Judah God is known; His Name is Great in Israel. 2 In Salem also is His Tabernacle, and His Dwelling Place in Zion. 3 There He broke the arrows of the bow, the shield and sword of battle. Selah. Psalms 78:65: Then The Lord awoke as from sleep, like a mighty man who shouts because of wine. 66 And He beat back His enemies; He put them to 'A Perpetual Reproach.' 68 But chose The Tribe of Judah, Mount Zion which He loved. 69 And He built His Sanctuary like the heights, like the earth which He has established forever. 70 And He chose David His servant and took Him from the sheepfolds; 71 From following the ewes that had young He brought them, to 'Shepherd Jacob' His People, and Israel His Inheritance. 72 So He shepherded them according to the integrity of His heart and guided them by The Skillfulness of His Hands.

II Chronicles 29:6: "For our fathers have trespassed and done evil in The Eyes of The Lord our God; they have forsaken Him, have turned their faces away from the Dwelling Place of The Lord, and turn their back on Him." 8 "Therefore 'The Wrath of The Lord' fell upon Judah and Jerusalem, and He has given them up to trouble, to astonishment, and to jeering, as you see with your eyes." 9 "For indeed, because of 'This' our fathers have fallen by 'The Sword'; and our sons, our daughters, and our wives are in captivity." 10 "Now it is My heart to make A Covenant with The Lord God of Israel, that His Fierce Wrath may turn away from us."

Habakkuk 2:2: Then The Lord answered Me and said: "Write The Vision and make it plain on tablets, that he may run who reads it." 20 "But The Lord is in His Holy Temple. Let all the earth keep silence before Him." 3:16: When I heard, My body trembled; My lips quivered at "The Voice," rottenness entered My bones; and I trembled in Myself, That I might rest in The Day of Trouble. When He comes up to the people, He will invade them with His Troops. 18 Yet I will rejoice in The Lord, I will joy in The God of My Salvation.

Hebrews 2:1: Therefore we must give 'The More Earnest Heed' to the things we have heard, lest we drift away. 2 For if 'The Word' spoken through angels proved steadfast, and every transgression and disobedience received 'A Just Reward.' 3 How shall we escape if we neglect so great 'A Salvation,' which at first began to be spoken by The Lord and was confirmed to us by those who heard Him, 13 And again: "I will put My trust in Him." And again: "Here Am I and the children whom God has given Me."

4:7: Again He designates 'A Certain Day,' saying in David, "TODAY," after such a long time, as it has been said: "Today, if you will hear 'His

Voice,' do not harden your hearts." 13 And there is no creature hidden from His Sight, but all things are naked and open to The Eyes of Him to whom we must give account. 6:11: And we desire that each one of you show the same diligence to the full assurance of hope until the end.

Daniel 7:2: Daniel spoke, saying, "I saw in my vision by night, and behold, the four winds of heaven were stirring up The Great Sea." 9 "I watched till thrones were put in place, and The Ancient of Days was seated; His garment was white as snow, and the hair of His head was like pure wool. His throne was a fiery flame, its wheels a burning fire. 10 A fiery stream issued and came forth from before Him. A thousand thousand ministered to Him; ten thousand times ten thousand stood before Him. The court was seated, and The Books were opened.

Daniel 8:19: And He said, "Look, I Am making known to You what shall happen in 'The Latter Time' of The Indignation; for at The Appointed Time 'The End' shall be." 9:13: "As it is written in The Law of Moses, all this disaster has come upon us; yet we have not made our prayer before The Lord our God, that we might turn from our iniquities and understand 'Your Truth.'" 14 "Therefore The Lord has kept the disaster in mind, and brought it upon us; for The Lord our God is righteous in all the works which He does, though we have not obeyed His Voice." 10:7: And I, Daniel, alone saw the vision for the men who were with Me did not see the vision; but a great terror fell upon them, so that they fled to hide themselves.

Daniel 10:11: And He said to Me, "O Daniel, man greatly beloved, understand The Words that I speak to You, and stand Upright, for I have been sent to You." While He was speaking This Word to Me, I stood trembling. 12 Then He said to Me, "Do not fear, Daniel, for from the first day that You set Yor Heart to understand, and to humble Yourself before Your God, your Words were heard; and I have come Because of Your Words."

Daniel 12:1: "At 'That Time' Michael shall stand up, The Great Prince who stands watch over the sons of your people; and there shall be A Time of Trouble, such as never was since there was a nation, even to 'That Time,' and at 'That Time' your people shall be delivered, Everyone who is found in "The Book." 4 "But You, Daniel, shut up 'The Words,' and seal 'The Book' until The Time of The End; many shall run to and fro, and knowledge shall increase." 13 "But You, go

Your Way till "The End'; for You shall rest, and will Arise to Your Inheritance at 'The End of The Days.'"

Jeremiah 36:2: "Take A Scroll of a book and write on it all 'The Words' that I have spoken to You against Israel, against Judah, and against 'All The Nations,' from the day I spoke to You, from the days of Josiah 'Even To This Day.' 6 "You go, therefore, and read from 'The Scroll' which You have written at My Instruction, "The Words of The Lord," in the hearing of The People in The Lord's House on The Day of Fasting. And You shall also read them in the hearing of all Judah who comes from their cities." 7 "It may be that they will present their supplication before The Lord, and Every One will turn from his evil way. For 'Great' is The Anger and The Fury that The Lord has pronounced against this people."

Ecclesiastes 1:1: The Words of The Preacher, The Son of David, King in Jerusalem. 12 I, The Preacher, was King over Israel in Jerusalem. 8:2: I say, "Keep 'The King's Commandment' for The Sake of Your Oath to God. 4 Where 'The Word' of A King is; there is power; and who may say to Him, "What are you doing?" 5 He who keeps His Command will experience nothing harmful; and A Wise Man's heart discerns both Time and Judgment, 6 Because for every matter there is Time and Judgment, though the misery of man increases greatly. 7 For he does not know what will happen; so who can tell him when it will occur?

Daniel 7:22: "Until 'The Ancient of Days' came, and A Judgment was made in favor of The Saints of 'The Most High,' and 'The Time' came for The Saints to possess 'The Kingdom.'" 27 Then 'The Kingdom' and dominion, and The Greatness of The Kingdoms under the whole heaven, shall be given to The People, The Saints of The Most High. His Kingdom is 'An Everlasting Kingdom,' and all dominions shall serve and obey Him. Revelation 22:3: And there shall be no more curse, but The Throne of God and of The Lamb shall be in it, and His servants shall serve Him. 4 They shall see His Face, and His name shall be on their foreheads.

Zephaniah 1:14: The Great Day of The Lord is near; it is near and hastens quickly. The noise of The Day of The Lord is bitter; there the mighty men shall cry out. 15 'That Day' is A Day of Wrath, a day of trouble and distress, a day of devastation and desolation, a day of darkness and gloominess, a day of clouds and thick darkness. 16 A day of Trumpet and alarm against the fortified cities and against the high towers.

Zechariah 12:7: "The Lord will save The Tents of Judah first, so that The Glory of the House of David and The Glory of The Inhabitants of Jerusalem shall not become greater than that of Judah. 8 In 'That Day' The Lord will defend The Inhabitants of Jerusalem; the one who is feeble among them in 'That Day' shall be like David, and The House of David shall be like God, like The Angel of The Lord before them." 13:1: "In 'That Day' A Fountain shall be opened for The House of David and for The Inhabitants of Jerusalem, for sin and for uncleanness." 2 "It shall be in 'That Day,'" says The Lord of hosts, "that I will cut off the names of the idols from the land, and they shall no longer be remembered. I will also cause the prophets and the unclean spirit to depart from the land."

Psalms 1:5: Therefore the ungodly shall not stand in The Judgment, nor sinners in The Congregation of The Righteous. 6 For The Lord knows 'The Way' of The Righteous, but the way of the ungodly shall perish. 2:5: Then He shall speak to them in His Wrath, and distress them in His deep displeasure: 9 You shall break them with a rod of iron; You shall dash them to pieces like a potter's vessel.

Psalms 4:6: There are many who say, "Who will show us any good?" Lord, lift up The Light of Your Countenance upon us. 7 You have put gladness in My heart, more than in the season that their grain and wine increased. 8 I will both lie down in peace, and sleep; for You alone, O Lord, make Me dwell in safety. 5:4: For You are not a God who takes pleasure in wickedness, nor shall evil dwell with You. 5 The boastful shall not stand in Your Sight; You hate all workers of iniquity. 6 You shall destroy those who speak falsehood; The Lord abhors the bloodthirsty and deceitful man. Psalms 21:11: For they intended evil against You; they devised a plot which they are not able to perform.

22:16: For dogs have surrounded Me; the congregation of the wicked has enclosed Me. They pierced My hands and My feet; 18 They divide My garments among them, and for My clothing they cast lots. 22 I will declare Your Name to My brethren; in the of The Assembly, I will praise You. 28 For 'The Kingdom' is The Lord's, and He rules over the nations. 31 They will 'Come' and 'Declare' His Righteousness to A People who will be Born, that He has done 'This.'

Genesis 1:1: In 'The Beginning' God created the heavens and the earth. 27 So God created man in His own image; in The Image of God He created him; male and female He created them. John 1:11: He came to His own, and His own did not receive Him. 13 Who were 'Born,' not of blood, nor of the will of the flesh, nor of the will of man, but of God. 14 And 'The Word' became flesh and dwelt among us, and we beheld His Glory, The Glory as of The Only Begotten of The Father, full of grace and Truth. Isaiah 2:5: O House of Jacob, 'Come' and let us walk in The Light of The Lord.

Isaiah 6: For You have forsaken Your people, The House of Jacob, because they are filled with eastern ways; they are soothsayers like the Philistines, and they are pleased with the children of foreigners. 7 Their land is also full of silver and gold, and there is no end to their treasures; their land is also full of horses, and there is no end to their chariots. 8 Their land is also full of idols; they worship the works of their own hands, that which their own fingers have made. 18 But the idols He shall utterly abolish.

Jeremiah 2:9: "Therefore I will yet bring charges against you," says The Lord, "And against your children's children I will bring charges." 10 For pass beyond the coasts of Cyprus and see, send to Kedar and consider diligently, and see if there has been such a thing. 14 "Is Israel a servant?" Is he a homeborn slave? Why is he plundered? 17 Have you not brought 'This' on yourself, in that you have forsaken The Lord Your God when He led you in 'The Way'?

3:21: A Voice was heard on the desolate heights, weeping and supplication of The Children of Israel. For they have perverted their way; they have forgotten The Lord their God. 23 Truly, in vain is Salvation hoped for from the hills, and from the multitude of mountains; truly, in The Lord our God is The Salvation of Israel. 25 We lie down in our shame, and our reproach covers us. For we have sinned against The Lord our God, we and our fathers, from our youth even to 'This Day,' and have not obeyed The Voice of The Lord Our God.

Jeremiah 4:5: Declare in Judah and proclaim in Jerusalem and say: "Blow the trumpet in the land; cry, 'Gather together,' and say, 'Assemble yourselves, and let us go into the fortified cities.' 6 Set up the standard toward Zion. Take refuge! Do not delay! For I will bring disaster from the north, and great destruction." 7 The Lion has come up from His thicket, and The Destroyer of Nations is on His Way. He has gone forth from His Place to make your land desolate. Your cities will be laid waste, without inhabitant.

11 At 'That Time' it will be said to this people and to Jerusalem, "A Dry Wind of the desolate heights blows in the wilderness toward The Daughter of My People—not to fan or to cleanse—12 A Wind too strong for these will come for Me; Now I will also speak judgment against them." 13 "Behold, He shall come up like clouds, and His chariots like a whirlwind. His horses are swifter than eagles. Woe to us, for we are plundered!"

Psalms 32:6: For 'This Cause' everyone who is godly shall pray to You in a time when You may be found; surely in a flood of great waters they shall not come near Him. 7 You are My Hiding Place, You shall preserve Me from trouble; You shall surround Me with 'Songs of Deliverance.' Selah. 11 Be glad in The Lord and rejoice, you are righteous; and shout for joy, all you 'Upright In Heart'! Psalms 33:4: For 'The Word of The Lord' is Right, and all His Work is done in Truth.

Daniel 9:1: In the first year of Darius the son of Ahasuerus, of the lineage of the Medes, who was made king over The Realm of the Chaldeans—2 In the first year of his reign I, Daniel, understood by The Books the number of the years specified by The Word of The Lord through Jeremiah the prophet, that He would accomplish seventy years in The Desolations of Jerusalem. 3 Then I set My Face toward The Lord God to make request by Prayer and Supplications, with fasting, sackcloth and ashes.

22 And He informed Me, and talked with Me, and said, "O Daniel, I have now come forth to give you skill to understand. 23 "At the beginning of Your supplications The Command went out, and I have come to tell You, for You are greatly beloved; therefore consider the matter, and 'Understand The Vision': 24 "Seventy weeks are determined for Your People and for Your Holy City, to finish the transgression, to make an end of sins, to make reconciliation for iniquity, to bring in 'Everlasting 'Righteousness,' to 'Seal Up' "Vision and Prophecy," and 'To Anoint The Most Holy.'" Joel 2:1: Blow the trumpet in Zion and sound an alarm in My Holy Mountain! Let all the inhabitants of the land tremble; for The Day of The Lord is coming, for it is at hand.

Revelation 22:6: Then He said to Me, "These Words are 'Faithful and True.'" And The Lord God of the holy prophets sent His Angel to show His servants the things which must shortly take place. 16 "I, Jesus, have sent My Angel to testify to you 'These Things' in the churches. I Am 'The Root and The Offspring of David,' 'The Bright And Morning Star.'" 17 And 'The Spirit' and The Bride say, "Come!" And let him who hears say, "Come!" And let him who thirsts Come. Whoever desires, let him take The Water of Life freely."

Ezekiel 34:24: "And I, The Lord, will be their God, and My Servant David a prince among them; I, The Lord, have spoken." 25 "I will make A Covenant of Peace with them, and cause wild beasts to cease from the land; and they will dwell safely in the wilderness and sleep in the woods." 26 "I will make them and the places all around My Hill a blessing; and I will cause showers to come down in their season; there shall be 'Showers of Blessing.'" 27 "Then the trees of the field shall yield their fruit, and the earth shall yield her increase. They shall be safe in their land; and they shall know that I Am The Lord, when I have broken the bands of their yoke and delivered them from the hand of those who enslaved them."

Zechariah 8:23: "Thus says The Lord of Hosts: 'In those days 'Ten Men' from every language of the nations shall grasp The Sleeve of A Jewish Man," saying, "Let us go with You, for we have heard that God is With You." 10:8: I will whistle for them and Gather Them, for I Will Redeem Them; and they shall increase as they once increased." 9 "I will show them among the peoples, and they shall remember Me in far countries; they shall live, together with their children, and they shall 'Return.'

Lamentations 3:40: Let us search out and examine our ways and turn back to The Lord. 42 We have transgressed and rebelled; You have not pardoned. 46 All our enemies have opened their mouths against us. 47 Fear and a snare have come upon us, desolation and destruction. 57 You drew near on 'The Day' I called on You, and said, "Do not fear!" 58 O Lord, You have pleaded The Case of My soul; You have redeemed My Life. Mark 4:14: "The Sower Sows 'The Word.'" 20 "But these are The Ones Sown on Good Ground, those who Hear 'The Word,' accept it, and bear fruit: some thirtyfold, some sixty, and some a hundred." 22 "For there is nothing hidden which will not be revealed, nor has anything been kept secret but that it should Come To Light."

I Corinthians 9:14: Even so The Lord has commanded that those who preach 'The Gospel' shall live from 'The Gospel.' 19 For though I Am free from all men, I have made Myself a servant to all, that I might 'Win The More'; 10:29: "Conscience," I say, not your own, but that of the other. For why is My Liberty judged by another man's conscience?

Galatians 1:15: But when it pleased God, who separated Me from My mother's womb and 'Called Me' through His Grace. 16 To reveal His Son in Me, that I might preach Him among the Gentiles, I did not immediately confer with flesh and blood, Ephesians 2:10: For we are His Workmanship, created in Christ Jesus for 'Good Works,' which God prepared beforehand that we should walk in them. 18 For through Him we both have access by One Spirit to The Father. 20 Having been built on The Foundation of The Apostles and Prophets, Jesus Christ Himself being 'The Chief Cornerstone.'

Ephesians 3:3: How that by Revelation He made known to Me 'The Mystery' (as I have written briefly already. 4 By which, when you read, you may understand My Knowledge in 'The Mystery of Christ'). 8 To Me, who am less than the least of all The Saints, This Grace was Given, that I should preach among the Gentiles 'The Unsearchable Riches of Christ'; 9 And to make 'All See' what is 'The Fellowship of The Mystery,' which from The Beginning of the ages has been 'Hidden in God' who created all things through Jesus Christ; 4:14: That we should no longer be children, tossed to and fro and carried about with every wind of doctrine, by the trickery of men, in the cunning craftiness of deceitful plotting, 18 Having their understanding darkened, being alienated from 'The Life of Christ,' because of the ignorance that is in them, because of the blindness of their heart.

Isaiah 24:17: Fear and The Pit and The Smear are upon you, O Inhabitant of The Earth. 28:22: Now therefore, do not be mockers, lest your bonds be made strong; for I have heard from The Lord God of hosts, a destruction determined even upon the whole earth. Habakkuk 1:3: Why do you show me iniquity, and cause Me to see trouble? For plundering and violence are before Me; there is strife, and contention arises. 5 "Look among the nations and Watch—be utterly astounded! For I will 'work a work' in 'Your Days' which you would not believe, though it were told you." Isaiah 33:2: O Lord, be gracious to us; we have waited for You. Be their arm every morning, our salvation also in time of trouble.

Isaiah 41:21: "Present Your Case," says The Lord, "Bring forth your strong reasons," says The King of Jacob. Isaiah 42:5: Thus says God The Lord, who created the heavens and stretched them out, who spread forth the earth and that which comes from it, who gives Breath to the people on it, and Spirit to those who walk on it: Isaiah 44:18: They do not know nor understand; for He has shut their eyes, so they cannot see, and their hearts, so that they cannot understand. 22 I have blotted out, like a thick cloud, your transgressions, and like a cloud, your sins, 'Return to Me,' for I have Redeemed you."

23 Sing, O heavens, for The Lord has done it! Shout, you lower parts of the earth; break forth into singing, your mountains, O forest, and every tree in it! for The Lord has redeemed Jacob and glorified Himself in Israel. 25 Who frustrates the signs of the babblers and drives diviners mad; who turns wise men backward and makes their knowledge foolishness; Isaiah 45:16: They shall be ashamed and also disgraced, all of them; they shall go in confusion together, who are makers of idols. 47:13: You are wearied in the multitude of your counsels; let now the astrologers, the stargazers, and the monthly prognosticators stand up and save you from what shall come upon you.

Romans 2:13 (For not the hearers of The Law are just in The Sight of God, but 'The Doers' of The Law will be justified; 14 For when Gentiles, who do not have The Law, by nature do the things in The Law, these, not having The Law, are a law to themselves, 15 Who show the work of The Law written in their hearts, their conscience also bearing witness, and between themselves their thoughts 'accusing or else excusing them').

16 In 'The Day' when God will judge the secrets of men by Jesus Christ, according to My Gospel. Romans 10:14: How then shall they call on Him in whom they do not believed? And how shall they believe in Him whom they have not heard? And how shall they hear without 'A Preacher'? 15 And how shall they preach unless they are Sent? As it is written: "How beautiful are the feet of those who preach The Gospel of Peace, who bring glad tidings of Good Things!"

Lamentations 3:1: I Am the man who has seen affliction by The Rod of His Wrath. 2 He has led me and made me walk in darkness and not in light. 3 Surely, He has turned His Hand against me time and time again throughout the day. 5 He has besieged me and surrounded me with bitterness and woe. 6 He has set me in dark places like the dead of long ago. 39 Why should A Living Man complain, A Man for The Punishment of His Sins?

Philippians 1:12: But I want you to know, brethren, that the things which happened to me have actually turned out for The Furtherance of The Gospel. 21 For to me, to live is Christ, and to die is gain. 23 For I Am hard pressed between the two, having the desire to depart and be with Christ, which is far better. 24 Nevertheless to remain is more needful for you.

Colossians 1:3: We give thanks to The God and Father of our Lord Jesus Christ, praying always for you, 4 Since we heard of your faith in Christ Jesus and of your love for all the saints; 5 Because of The Hope which is laid up for you in heaven, of which you heard before in The Word of The Truth of The Gospel, I Thessalonians 2:13: For 'This' reason we also Thank God without ceasing, because when you received 'The Word of God' which you heard from us, you welcomed it Not as the word of man, but as it is in Truth, The Word of God, which also effectively works in you who believe.

Galatians 3:5: Therefore He who supplies The Spirit to you and works miracles among you, does He do it by The Works of The Law, or by The Hearing of Faith? 8 And The Scripture, foreseeing that God would justify the Gentiles by faith, preached The Gospel to Abraham beforehand, saying, "In You all the nations shall be blessed." Colossians 1:26: 'The Mystery' which has been hidden from ages and from generations, but 'Now' has been revealed to His Saints.

28 Him we preach, warning every man and teaching every man in 'All Wisdom,' that we may present every man perfect in Christ Jesus. 29 To 'This End' I also labor, striving according to His Working which works in Me mightily. II Timothy 2:19: Nevertheless 'The Solid Foundation of God' stands, having 'This Seal': "The Lord knows those who are His," and "Let everyone who Names 'The Name of Christ' depart from iniquity." 4:17: But The Lord stood with Me and strengthened Me, so that 'The Message' might be preached fully through Me, and that all the Gentiles might hear. Also I was delivered out of the mouth of the lion. Daniel 6:22: "My God sent His Angels and shut the lions' mouths, so that they have not hurt Me, because 'I Was Found Innocent' before Him; and also, O king, I have done no wrong before you."

Joel 2:11: The Lord gives Voice before His army, for His camp is very great; for strong is 'The One' who executes 'His Word.' For The Day of The Lord is great and very terrible; Who can endure it? 32 And it shall come to pass that whoever calls on The Name of The Lord shall be saved. For in Mount Zion and in Jerusalem there shall be 'Deliverance, as The Lord has said, among 'The Remnant Whom The Lord Calls.' 3:16: The Lord also will roar from Zion, and utter 'His Voice' from Jerusalem; the heavens and earth will shake; but The Lord shall be a shelter for 'His People,' and The Strength of The Children of Israel.

Amos 3:7: Surely The Lord God does nothing, unless he reveals His Secret to His servants the prophets. 4:13: For behold, He who forms mountains, and creates the wind, who declares to man what 'His Thought' is, and makes the morning darkness, who treads the high places of the earth—The Lord God of host is His Name. Exodus 34:10: And He said: "Behold, I make A Covenant. Before all your people I will do marvels such as have not been done in all the earth, nor in any nation; and all the people among whom you are shall see The Work of The Lord. For it is an awesome thing that I will do with you."

Numbers 23:19: "God is not a man, that He should lie, nor a son of man, that He should repent. Has He said, and will He not do? Or has He spoken, and will He not make it good?" Galatians 3:16: Now to Abraham and his Seed were The Promises made. He does not say, "And to seeds," as of many, but as of one, "And to your Seed," who is Christ. 19 What purposes then does The Law serve? It was added because of transgressions, till 'The Seed' should come "To Whom' The Promise was made; and it was appointed through angels by The Hand of The Mediator. 21 Is The Law then against The Promises of God? Certainly not! For if there had been A Law given which could have given Life, Truly Righteousness would have been by The Law. 24 Therefore The Law was our tutor to bring us to Christ, that we might be justified by faith.

I Thessalonians 4:8: Therefore he who rejects 'This' does not reject man, but God, who has also given us 'His Holy Spirit.' Isaiah 1:12: "When you come to appear before Me, who has required 'This' from your hand, to trample My Courts." 18 "Come Now, and let us reason together," says The Lord. "Though your sins are like scarlet, they shall be ae white as snow; though they are like red crimson, they shall be as wool. 19 If you are willing and obedient, you shall eat The Good of

The Land. 20 But if you refuse and rebel, you shall be devoured by 'The Sword'"; for The Mouth of The Lord Has Spoken.

Ecclesiastes 2:24: Nothing is better for a man than that he should eat and drink, and that his soul should enjoy good in his labor. This also, I saw, was from The Hand of God. 3:11: He has made everything beautiful in its time. Also, He has put eternity in their hearts, except that no one can find out The Work that God does from Beginning to End. 12 I know that nothing is better for them than to rejoice, and to do good in their lives, 14 I know that whatever God does, it shall be forever. Nothing can be added to it, and nothing taken from it. God does it, that men should fear before Him.

Ecclesiastes 7:18: It is that you grasp 'This,' and also not remove your hand from the other; For He Who 'Fears God' will escape them all. 27 "Hear is what I have found," says The Preacher, "Adding 'One Thing' to the other to find out 'The Reason,' Matthew 1:22: So 'All This' was done that it might be fulfilled which was spoken by The Lord through the prophets, saying: 23 "Behold, the virgin shall be with child, and bear a Son, and they shall call His Name Immanuel," which is translated, "God With Us."

Luke 1:32: "He will be great and will be called 'The Son of The Highest'; and The Lord God will give Him The Throne of His Father David." 33 "And He will reign over The House of Jacob forever, and His Kingdom there will be no end." 37 "For with God nothing will be impossible." 50 And His Mercy is on those who 'Fear Him' from generation to generation. 2:23: (As it is written in The Law of The Lord, "Every male who opens the womb shall be called Holy to The Lord").

Ephesians 6:11: Put on The Whole Armor of God, that you may be able to stand against the wiles of the devil. 12 For we do not wrestle against flesh and blood, but against principalities, against powers, against the rulers of darkness of 'This Age,' against spiritual hosts of wickedness in the heavenly places. 13 Therefore take up The Whole Armor of God, that you may be able to withstand in the evil day, and having done all, to stand.

14 Stand therefore, having girded your waist with Truth, having put on The Breastplate of Righteousness. 15 And having shod your feet with the preparation of The Gospel of Peace; 16 Above all, taking The

Shield of Faith with which, you will be able to Quench all the fiery darts of the wicked one. 17 And take The Helmet of Salvation, and The Sword of The Spirit, which is "The Word of God."

II John 1:7: For many deceivers have gone out into the world who do not confess Jesus Christ as coming in the flesh. This is a deceiver and an anti-Christ. 9 Whoever transgresses and does not abide in The Doctrine of Christ does not have God. He who abides in The Doctrine of Christ has both The Father and The Son.

Psalms 84:1: How lovely is Your Tabernacle, O Lord of Hosts! 2 My soul longs, yes, even faints for The Courts of The Lord; My heart and My flesh cry out for 'The Living God.' 3 Even the sparrow has found a home, and the swallow a nest for herself, where she may lay her young—even Your altars, O Lord of Hosts, My King and My God. 4 Blessed are those who dwell in Your House; they will still be praising You. Selah.

5 Blessed is the man whose strength is in You, whose heart is set on Pilgrimage. 6 As they pass through the valley of Baca, they make it a spring; the rain also covers it with pools. 7 They go from strength to strength; "Each One Appears Before God In Zion." 8 O Lord God of Hosts, Hear My Prayer; give ear, O God of Jacob! Selah.

9 O God, behold Our Shield, and look upon The Face of Your Anointed. 10 For 'A Day' in Your Courts is better than a thousand. I would rather be 'A Doorkeeper' in The House of My God than dwell on the tents of wickedness. 11 For God is a Sun and Shield; The Lord will give grace and glory; no good thing will be withheld from those who walk Uprightly. 12 O Lord of Hosts blessed is the man who trusts in You!

@MEM

Psalms 119:97: Oh. how I love Your Law! It is 'My Meditation' all the day. 98 You, through Your Commandments, make Me Wiser than My enemies; for They are ever with Me. 99 I have more understanding than all My teachers, for Your Testimonies are 'My Meditation.' 100 I understand more than The Ancients, because I keep Your Precepts. 101 I have restrained My feet from every evil way, that I may keep 'Your Word.' 102 I have not departed from Your Judgments, for You Yourself have 'Taught Me.' 103 How sweet are Your Words to My taste, sweeter than honey to My Mouth! 104 Through Your Precepts I get understanding; therefore, I hate every false way.

John 1:1: In 'The Beginning' was "The Word," and "The Word" was with God, and "The Word" was God. 14 And 'The Word' became flesh and dwelt among us, and we beheld 'His Glory,' The Glory as of The Only Begotten of The Father, Full of Grace and Truth. 17 For 'The Law' was given through Moses, but Grace and Truth came through Jesus Christ. 19 Now this is 'The Testimony of John,' when the Jews sent priests and Levites from Jerusalem to ask him, "Who are you?" 23 He said: "I Am 'The Voice of 'One' crying in the wilderness: "Make straight The Way of The Lord,"' as the prophet Isaiah said." 26 John answered them, saying, "I baptize with water, but 'There Stands One' among you whom you do not know." 29 The next day John saw Jesus coming toward him, and said, "Behold! The Lamb of God who takes away the sin of the world!" 34 "And I have seen and testified that This is The Son of God."

John 3:11: "Most assuredly, I say to you, We speak what We know and Testify what We have seen, and you do not receive Our Witness." 12 "If I have told you earthly things and you do not believe, how will you believe if I tell you heavenly things?" 13 "No one has ascended to heaven but He who came down from heaven, that is, The Son of Man who is in heaven." 14 "And as Moses lifted up the serpent in the wilderness, even so must The Son of Man be lifted up." 15 "That whoever believes in Him should not perish but have Eternal Life."

29 "He who has 'The Bride' is 'The Bridegroom'; but the friend of 'The Bridegroom,' who stands and 'Hears Him,' rejoices greatly because 'The Bridegroom's Voice.' Therefore 'This Joy of Mine' is fulfilled." 34 "For He whom 'God Has Sent' speaks 'The Word of God,' For God does not give 'The Spirit' by measure." 35 "The Father loves The Son, and has given all things into 'His Hand.'" 36 "He who believes in 'The Son' has everlasting life; and he who does not believe 'The Son' shall not see life, but The Wrath of God abides on him."

John 5:39: "You search The Scriptures, for in 'Them' you think you have Eternal Life; and these are they which 'Testify of Me.'" 40 "But you are not willing to 'Come To Me' that you may have 'Life.' 6:37 "All that 'The Father' gives Me will 'Come To Me,' and the one who 'Comes To Me' I will by no means cast out." 39 "This is 'The Will of The Father' who Sent Me, that of all He has Given Me I should lose nothing, but should 'Raise It Up' at 'The Last Day.'" 45 "It is written in the prophets, 'And they shall all be taught by God,' Therefore everyone 'Who Has Heard and Learned' from The Father 'Comes To Me.'" 63 "It is 'The Spirit' who gives Life, the flesh profits nothing. 'The Words' that I speak to you are 'Spirit,' and 'They Are Life.'"

II Kings 22:13: "Go, inquire of The Lord for Me, for The People and for all Judah, concerning The Words of 'This Book' that has been found; for 'Great' is The Wrath of The Lord that is aroused against us, because our fathers have not obeyed The Words of 'This Book,' to do according to All that is written concerning us."

I Thessalonians 5:19: "Do not quench The Spirit. 20 Do not despise prophecies. 21 Test all things; hold fast what is good. 22 Abstain from every form of evil. 24 He who calls you is faithful, who also will "Do It." 27 I charge you by The Lord that this Epistle Be read to all The Holy Brethren."

Isaiah 45:15: Truly You are God, who hides Yourself, O God of Israel, 'The Savior'! 16 They shall be ashamed and also disgraced, all of them; they shall go in confusion together, who are makers of idols. 17 But Israel shall be 'Saved' by The Lord with 'An Everlasting Salvation'; you shall not be ashamed or disgraced forever and ever. 18 For 'Thus Says The Lord,' who created the heavens, who is God, who formed the earth and made it, and who has established it, who did not create it in vain, who formed it to be inhabited: "I Am The Lord, and there is no other." 22 Look to Me, and be 'Saved,' all you ends of the earth! For I Am God and there is no other. 23 "I have sworn by Myself; 'The Word' has gone out of My Mouth in righteousness, and shall not return, that to Me every knee shall bow, every tongue shall take 'An Oath.'"

Revelation 19:6: And I heard, as it were, 'The Voice' of a great multitude, as the sound of many waters and as the sound of mighty thundering, saying "ALLELUIA! FOR THE LORD GOD OMNIPOTENT REIGNS!" 7 "Let us be glad and rejoice and give Him glory, for 'The Marriage of The Lamb has come,' and His wife has made herself ready." 10 And I fell at His feet to 'Worship Him.' But He said to Me, "See that you do not do that! I Am your fellow servant, and of 'Your Brethren' who have 'The Testimony of Jesus.' "WORSHIP GOD!" For 'The Testimony of Jesus' is The Spirit of Prophecy." 22:20: He who testifies "These Things" says, "Surely I am coming quickly." Amen. Even so, Come, Lord Jesus! 21 The Grace of our Lord Jesus Christ be with you all. Amen.